Smalltalk Mastery
An In-Depth Exploration and Practical Handbook

Adam Jones

Contents

Preface

Welcome to "Smalltalk Mastery: An In-Depth Exploration and Practical Handbook." This book is crafted to deliver a comprehensive and insightful journey into the world of Smalltalk programming—an iconic language that has significantly influenced modern software development paradigms. Whether you are stepping into the realm of programming for the first time or are a seasoned developer eager to explore Smalltalk's distinctive methodologies, this handbook promises a rich and rewarding exploration.

The essence of this book lies in demystifying Smalltalk, a pioneering object-oriented programming language that embodies simplicity, uniformity, and an elegant craftsmanship of coding. Our goal is to present Smalltalk not only as a tool for coding but as a philosophy of design that encourages creativity, clarity, and adaptability. Each chapter of this book is meticulously crafted to build your knowledge progressively, offering a blend of theoretical insights and practical, hands-on learning experiences.

In "Smalltalk Mastery," you'll find a structured path that guides you from the core principles of Smalltalk to advanced programming techniques. Initially, we focus on the foundational elements, such as syntax and basic object-oriented concepts. As you progress, we delve into complex areas like error handling, debugging, and performance optimization. Additionally, distinct chapters are dedicated to exploring graphical user interface programming with Morphic, and crafting modern web applications using the powerful Seaside framework.

These topics are illustrated with detailed examples and industry best practices, ensuring you gain a robust, applicable understanding.

This book does more than just impart technical skills; it encourages an appreciation for Smalltalk's underlying principles—the elegant leveraging of code brevity, the beauty of a unified object model, and the expressive power of messaging between objects. By mastering these aspects, you'll be equipped to design and develop software solutions that are not only effective but also inherently elegant and sustainable.

Our target audience extends across a spectrum of learners. Beginners who have grasped the rudiments of programming in other languages will find our introductory chapters to Smalltalk's unique features particularly enlightening. Meanwhile, more seasoned developers will be challenged and engaged by the in-depth analysis of Smalltalk's sophisticated constructs and the exploration of its applicable power in creating novel software solutions.

"Smalltalk Mastery: An In-Depth Exploration and Practical Handbook" aspires to be more than just a guide; it is an invitation to experience Smalltalk as a transformative way of thinking about code and systems. As you delve into its pages, you'll uncover not only the technicalities required to master Smalltalk but also a deeper appreciation for its aesthetic simplicity and timeless relevance in the ever-evolving landscape of programming languages. By the conclusion of this handbook, our ambition is for you to emerge not merely as a user of Smalltalk but as a master of its distinguished artistry.

Chapter 1

Introduction to Smalltalk

Smalltalk stands as one of the pioneers in the realm of object-oriented programming languages, introducing concepts that have significantly influenced the development of modern software engineering. It has a distinct syntax and programming environment designed to enhance productivity and foster a more intuitive understanding of programming models. This chapter provides a gateway into the world of Smalltalk, covering its history, foundational principles, and the essentials of its programming environment. Through exploring these fundamental aspects, readers will gain an appreciation for Smalltalk's design philosophy and its role in shaping the landscape of object-oriented programming.

1.1 The Origins and History of Smalltalk

The inception of Smalltalk can be traced back to the early 1970s at the Xerox Palo Alto Research Center (PARC), an establishment renowned for its groundbreaking contributions to the field of computer science. Smalltalk was devised by a team led by Alan Kay, who envisioned a programming language that embodied the principle of "objects" –

a concept that later became a cornerstone in the domain of object-oriented programming (OOP).

Smalltalk's development was influenced by Kay's desire to create a system that was not only intuitive for professional programmers but also accessible to novice users, including children. He drew inspiration from the Dynabook concept, a theoretical personal computer for children of all ages, conceptualizing a programming environment that supported an interactive and exploratory learning approach.

The initial versions of Smalltalk, namely Smalltalk-71 and Smalltalk-72, laid the foundation for what would become a revolutionary approach to software development. These early iterations introduced innovative ideas such as "message passing" between objects, but they were primarily experimental.

Significant progress was made with the release of Smalltalk-76, which introduced a more robust and comprehensive programming environment. This version, along with its successor, Smalltalk-80, which was released to the wider academic and professional community, established a blueprint for modern object-oriented programming languages. Smalltalk-80, in particular, was notable for its integrated development environment (IDE), comprising a compiler, class library, and tools that supported the graphical user interface (GUI) - a novel feature at that time.

The philosophy behind Smalltalk was not confined to the technical design of the language; it extended to how the language was perceived and interacted with by the user. Smalltalk was designed to be more than a tool for professional developers; it was an educational platform that encouraged exploration and experimentation. This philosophy is evident in the language's emphasis on simplicity and consistency in its design, which allows users to gradually discover and harness its capabilities.

Throughout the 1980s, Smalltalk's influence spread beyond its initial academic and research-based confines, finding applications in enterprise software development. Companies began to recognize the benefits of object-oriented programming, particularly in terms of code reuse and the ability to model complex systems. However, despite its pioneering role and influence on subsequent programming languages like Java and Python, Smalltalk's adoption in the industry has been overshadowed by these later languages.

In summary, the origins and historical development of Smalltalk highlight its pivotal role in shaping the landscape of object-oriented programming. From its conceptualization at Xerox PARC to its influence on contemporary software engineering practices, Smalltalk embodies a blend of technical innovation and a vision for a more intuitive and exploratory approach to computer programming. Its legacy continues to be celebrated within the programming community for its foundational contribution to the principles and practices of software development.

1.2 Philosophy and Principles behind Smalltalk

Smalltalk's philosophy revolves around the principles of simplicity, uniformity, and malleability. At its core, Smalltalk aims to provide a programming environment that mirrors the way humans think about and interact with the world, emphasizing objects and their interactions. This philosophy permeates every aspect of Smalltalk, from its syntax to its runtime environment, significantly distinguishing it from other programming languages.

The principle of simplicity is evident in Smalltalk's minimal syntax. Unlike languages that require extensive boilerplate code to perform simple tasks, Smalltalk was designed to be as concise and readable as possible. This design choice not only makes Smalltalk code easier to write and understand but also encourages programmers to focus on their problem-solving strategies rather than on the complexity of the language syntax.

```
"An example of Smalltalk code demonstrating its simplicity"
| myMessage |
myMessage := 'Hello, Smalltalk'.
Transcript show: myMessage.
```

In the code snippet above, a string is assigned to the variable myMessage and then printed to the Transcript, demonstrating Smalltalk's straightforward approach to variable declaration and output.

The uniformity principle in Smalltalk refers to the treatment of all elements as objects. This uniform object model is a fundamental aspect of Smalltalk, allowing a consistent way to interact with data and functionality. Everything in Smalltalk, from simple data types like integers and strings to more complex data structures and blocks of code, is treated as an object. This uniformity simplifies the programming model, as the same message-passing mechanism can be used to interact with any object, regardless of its complexity.

```
"An example demonstrating uniformity in Smalltalk"
| number1 number2 sum |
number1 := 5.
number2 := 10.
sum := number1 + number2.
Transcript show: sum printString.
```

In the example, both `number1` and `number2` are objects, and the addition operation is effectively a message passed between these objects, resulting in a new object `sum` that represents their sum.

Malleability, the third principle, emphasizes the extendibility and adaptability of the Smalltalk environment. Smalltalk was designed to be an open system where everything can be inspected, modified, and extended at runtime. This level of malleability fosters an exploratory programming approach, where developers can dynamically alter the behavior of the system to suit their needs, encouraging experimentation and rapid prototyping.

```
"An example illustrating malleability in Smalltalk"
Smalltalk at: #MyClass put: (Object subclass: #MyClass).
(Smalltalk at: #MyClass) addMethod: #myMethod with: ['This is malleable!'].
```

In this example, a new class `MyClass` is dynamically added to the Smalltalk environment, and a method `myMethod` is attached to it, demonstrating the dynamic nature of the language.

Understanding these three principles is crucial for grasifying the essence of Smalltalk and its approach to object-oriented programming. By embracing simplicity, uniformity, and malleability, Smalltalk offers a unique and powerful environment for software development, distinguishing it from other programming languages and paradigms.

1.3 Overview of Smalltalk Programming Environment

The Smalltalk programming environment is a comprehensive workspace designed to support the development of Smalltalk applications. Unlike traditional programming environments, Smalltalk's environment is fully integrated, meaning that the environment not only includes tools for writing code but also for debugging, testing, and deploying applications. This integration facilitates a seamless workflow from the initial design phase to the final deployment.

One of the hallmark features of the Smalltalk environment is its live object-oriented database. This means that all objects, including the code itself, are live and can be inspected, modified, and interacted with during the execution of a program. This dynamic aspect of Smalltalk allows developers to modify code on-the-fly and see the effects of changes immediately, without the need for recompilation. This feature underscores Smalltalk's emphasis on interactivity and immediate feedback, characteristics that are central to its design philosophy.

The environment is typically graphical, with a user interface that includes a code browser, a debugger, an object inspector, and tools for version control. Let's delve into each of these components:

- The `Code Browser` is a tool that allows developers to navigate through classes and methods in the system. It supports searching, browsing, and editing code. The browser's design makes it simple to find classes or methods by name, enabling developers to quickly locate and modify the parts of the system they are interested in.

- The Debugger in Smalltalk is a powerful tool for diagnosing and correcting errors in code. When a runtime error occurs, the debugger opens automatically, displaying the stack trace and providing direct access to the source code where the error occurred. Developers can inspect the state of objects, step through code execution, and make changes to fix errors directly within the debugger.

- The Object Inspector is a tool for examining and manipulating the state of objects at runtime. It provides a way to view the properties of an object, including its fields and methods, and to modify them if necessary. This tool embodies the principle of transparency and manipulation of live objects that is central to Smalltalk.

- Version Control Tools are integrated into the Smalltalk environment, assisting developers in managing changes to the codebase. These tools typically offer interfaces for committing changes, branching, merging, and viewing the history of modifications.

The configuration of the Smalltalk environment can vary depending on the implementation. Some versions are designed for specific platforms, while others aim for portability across different operating systems. Key implementations of Smalltalk, such as Squeak, Pharo, and VisualWorks, each provide their variation of the programming environment, with differences mostly in user interface design and additional tools available.

Here is an example of how a simple message can be sent to an object in the Smalltalk environment:

```
"Sending a message to an object"
Transcript show: 'Hello, world!'.
```

In this example, the 'Transcript' object, which represents a simple console or output stream, receives the message 'show:' with the argument ''Hello, world!''. The effect is to print the string 'Hello, world¡ to the Transcript, demonstrating how messages and objects interact in Smalltalk.

The output in the Transcript window would appear as follows:

```
Hello, world!
```

The Smalltalk programming environment is a rich and dynamic workspace designed around the principles of immediate feedback, transparency, and live interaction. Its tools and components work in unison to provide a seamless and interactive development experience, reflecting Smalltalk's philosophy of simplicity and directness.

1.4 Basic Syntax and Structure of Smalltalk Code

Smalltalk, with its emphasis on simplicity and uniformity, offers a syntax that is remarkably concise and readable. The language's syntax is centered around sending messages to objects. This approach is not only fundamental to understanding Smalltalk but also to mastering its application in object-oriented programming. In this section, we delve into the basic syntax and structural conventions of Smalltalk code, presenting key concepts through examples for clarity.

Comments

In Smalltalk, comments are enclosed within double quotes. This allows developers to include explanatory remarks or disable sections of code. Here is an example:

```
" This is a comment in Smalltalk "
```

Comments do not nest, and they can span multiple lines. Their usage is crucial for maintaining code clarity and aiding other developers or future self in understanding the rationale behind certain code segments.

Messages, Methods, and Blocks

Messages in Smalltalk can be thought of as method calls in other programming languages. There are three types of messages: unary, binary, and keyword messages.

- Unary messages: Involve a single object and do not require additional information.

```
array size.
```

- Binary messages: Operate on two objects and include operators such as +, -, <, >, etc.

```
5 + 3.
```

- Keyword messages: Include one or more keywords each followed by an argument.

```
Array new: 10.
```

A method in Smalltalk is a collection of statements that perform a task. Methods are always associated with a class and are invoked by sending a message to an object of that class.

Blocks are anonymous functions or closures. They are code blocks that can be passed around and executed. A block is enclosed in square brackets.

```
[ :x | x < 10 ]
```

This block takes a single argument x and evaluates whether x is less than 10.

Variables

Variables in Smalltalk are strictly typed as either instance variables, class variables, or local variables. Instance variables are unique to each instance of a class, class variables are shared across all instances of a class, and local variables exist within the scope of a method or block.

```
| myLocalVariable |
myLocalVariable := 5.
```

Here, `myLocalVariable` is a local variable assigned the value 5.

Control Structures

Smalltalk uses messages rather than traditional control structures seen in other languages. Conditional execution and loops are implemented using block structures.

```
true ifTrue: [ 'This will execute' ].
false ifFalse: [ 'This will also execute' ].

1 to: 5 do: [ :n |
    Transcript show: n printString; cr.
].
```

In the examples above, `ifTrue:` and `ifFalse:` are conditional messages, while `to:do:` is used to create a loop from 1 to 5, printing each number.

Putting It All Together

A simple example to illustrate these concepts is a Smalltalk program that calculates the factorial of a number.

```
factorial := [ :n |
    n <= 1 ifTrue: [ ^1 ].
    n * (factorial value: n - 1)
].

Transcript show: (factorial value: 5) printString; cr.
```

The `factorial` block takes a number `n` as input. If `n` is less than or equal to 1, it returns 1. Otherwise, it recursively calculates the factorial by sending the `value:` message to itself with `n - 1` as the argument. The result is printed to the Transcript, showing `120` for `n = 5`.

```
120
```

By dissecting the syntax and structure of Smalltalk code through these examples, readers gain a foundational understanding that facilitates their journey into more advanced topics and practical applications in Smalltalk programming.

1.5 Understanding Messages and Message Passing

Smalltalk's programming model is centered around the concept of objects communicating with one another through the passing of messages. This encapsulates one of the core principles of object-oriented programming, emphasizing that objects are autonomous entities that interact by sending messages to request actions.

In Smalltalk, every action is initiated by sending a message to an object. This includes performing operations, altering the object's state, or even querying the object for information. The syntax for message passing in Smalltalk illustrates this interaction in a straightforward manner.

Consider the scenario where one wants to add two numbers, say 3 and 5. In many programming languages, this operation might involve a direct expression like *3 + 5*. In Smalltalk, however, this operation is viewed as sending the message *+ 5* to the object *3*. This is expressed in Smalltalk syntax as below:

```
3 + 5.
```

This line of code demonstrates sending the + message, with *5* as its argument, to *3*. The result of this operation, if executed in a Smalltalk environment, is presented as:

```
8
```

Messages in Smalltalk can be categorized into three main types:

- Unary messages - These are messages that do not require any arguments. An example would be requesting the size of a collection.
- Binary messages - These involve two operands and include messages for mathematical operations and comparisons.
- Keyword messages - These messages include one or more arguments, each prefixed with a keyword to clarify the operation's intent.

For each message sent, the receiving object looks for a corresponding method that matches the message. If a matching method is found, the object executes the method's code with the supplied arguments if any.

The process of method lookup and execution can be formalized as follows. Given an object O and a message M, the sequence of actions is:

1. O searches for a method that matches M in its method list.
2. If O finds a matching method, O executes the method with any arguments passed along with M.
3. If no matching method is found, O follows its inheritance chain to look for the method.
4. If the method remains unfound, a *doesNotUnderstand:* message is sent to O.

This messaging system grants Smalltalk its dynamic behavior, allowing objects to respond to messages based on their current state and the methods they encapsulate. It embodies the principle that "everything is an object" and "every operation is a message pass", which are pivotal to Smalltalk's design philosophy and its approach to object-oriented programming.

In summary, understanding messages and message passing is crucial for programming in Smalltalk. It encourages developers to think in terms of objects and their interactions, rather than functions or procedures. This paradigm shift enhances modularity, encapsulation, and polymorphism, leading to more intuitive and flexible code.

1.6 Objects and Classes in Smalltalk

Objects form the cornerstone of Smalltalk's programming paradigm, encapsulating data and behavior in a harmonious structure. The object-oriented nature of Smalltalk is such that everything in the environment is treated as an object, from primitive data types such as numbers and strings to more complex structures like user interfaces and file systems. This unification under the object model facilitates a consistent and powerful approach to software design and development.

Classes in Smalltalk act as blueprints for objects. They define the structure and behavior that objects of that class will have. Each object is an instance of a class, inheriting its characteristics and capabilities. The class mechanism in Smalltalk not only provides a template for creating objects but also serves as a namespace wherein functions (known as methods in Smalltalk) that operate on these objects are defined.

Let's delve into the syntax and structure for defining a class in Smalltalk. A class is defined with keywords that specify its place in the class hierarchy, its instance variables (fields that store data unique to an object), and its methods. Below is a simplistic class definition in Smalltalk syntax:

```
Object subclass: #Dog
    instanceVariableNames: 'name breed'
    classVariableNames: ''
    poolDictionaries: ''
    category: 'Pets'.
```

In the above example, `Dog` is defined as a subclass of `Object`, indicating that `Dog` inherits behavior from `Object`, the root class of all objects in Smalltalk. The `instanceVariableNames` field lists the variables 'name' and 'breed' that will be unique to each instance of Dog. Following the class definition, methods that operate on instances of the class can be defined.

```
Dog >> bark
    ^'Woof! My name is ', self name, ' and I am a ', self breed, '.'.
```

This method, bark, when sent to a Dog object, returns a string containing the dog's name and breed. The self keyword is used to refer to the object the method is being called on, allowing access to its instance variables and other methods.

Smalltalk's messaging system is fundamental to how objects communicate and interact. Messages are sent to objects, and how the object responds is determined by its class's methods. For instance:

```
| myPet |
myPet := Dog new.
myPet name: 'Buddy'.
myPet breed: 'Golden Retriever'.
Transcript show: myPet bark.
```

In the above example, a new instance of Dog is created and stored in the variable myPet. The name: and breed: methods are used to set the dog's name and breed, respectively. The bark method is then invoked, and its return value is printed to the Transcript, which is Smalltalk's console/log. The expected output would be:

```
Woof! My name is Buddy and I am a Golden Retriever.
```

Inherently, Smalltalk promotes encapsulation and message-passing, with objects being the primary mechanism for both data storage and behavior encapsulation. Understanding and utilizing objects and classes are foundational in mastering Smalltalk, serving as the groundwork upon which the rest of Smalltalk's programming model is built.

1.7 Key Features of Smalltalk

Smalltalk is distinguished by several key features that not only set it apart from other programming languages but also contribute significantly to its enduring relevance in the field of software engineering. This section delineates these features, elucidating how they facilitate a distinctive programming experience and promote a deep understanding of object-oriented concepts.

- **Pure Object-Oriented Design:** Unlike many languages that support object-oriented programming to a certain degree alongside procedural paradigms, Smalltalk is purely object-oriented. Every entity in Smalltalk is an object, including numbers, characters, and even control structures. This consistency simplifies the learning curve for beginners and reinforces the principles of object-oriented programming throughout the development process.

- **Dynamic Typing:** Smalltalk employs dynamic typing rather than static typing. This means that the type of a variable is not fixed at compile time but is determined at runtime. This feature enhances flexibility and accelerates development because it allows for more generic code that can operate on diverse types of objects. However, it also necessitates a rigorous testing regime to prevent type-related errors.

- **Message Passing Syntax:** One of the most distinctive aspects of Smalltalk is its message-passing syntax. Objects communicate by sending messages to each other, which invokes methods on the receiving object. This syntax closely mimics natural language, making code more readable and expressive. For instance, to add two numbers, one would send a message to the first number, passing the second number as an argument:

```
result := 5 add: 3.
```

- **Integrated Development Environment (IDE):** Smalltalk provides a comprehensive IDE that integrates all aspects of software development, including writing, testing, and debugging code, as well as managing projects. This environment supports a highly interactive and iterative development process where changes can be made and tested on the fly.

- **Image-Based Persistence:** Instead of saving code in text files, Smalltalk uses an image file to store the entire state of the system, including both code and data. This approach enables a seamless transition between sessions, as developers can pick up exactly where they left off without the need to recompile code or reload data.
- **Reflective System:** Smalltalk is reflective, meaning that it can inspect and modify its own structure and behavior at runtime. This capability supports advanced features like dynamic code generation and modification, and introspection, making it possible to write highly dynamic and adaptive systems.
- **Garbage Collection:** Memory management in Smalltalk is automated through garbage collection. This process identifies and deallocates objects that are no longer in use, freeing developers from the burden of manual memory management and reducing the risk of memory leaks.

Each of these features contributes to a programming environment that is not only powerful and flexible but also uniquely conducive to a deep engagement with the principles of object-oriented design. Whether through its pure object-oriented approach, intuitive message-passing syntax, or comprehensive IDE, Smalltalk offers a coherent and holistic development experience that has influenced countless programmers and the design of numerous programming languages.

1.8 Smalltalk Development Tools and IDEs

For developers making their foray into Smalltalk, understanding the available Integrated Development Environments (IDEs) and tools is crucial. These IDEs are designed to provide robust support for coding, debugging, and testing Smalltalk-based applications, thereby significantly enhancing developer productivity and the overall software development process.

Smalltalk, by its nature, emphasizes an interactive development environment, combining code editing, compiling, debugging, and testing within a unified interface. This section will explore some of the prominent Smalltalk IDEs and tools that play a pivotal role in Smalltalk development.

Squeak/Pharo: Squeak is an open-source Smalltalk programming system that is highly portable and comes with its own integrated environment. Pharo, a fork of Squeak, aims at offering a more polished user interface and added functionalities, focusing on modern requirements. Both provide a self-contained development environment with sophisticated tools including a powerful code browser, testing frameworks, and refactoring tools.

- **Code Browsing and Editing:** Squeak / Pharo's code browser allows developers to easily navigate through classes and methods, making source code manipulation a breeze.
- **Debugger:** The debugger in these environments not only points to the source of an error but also allows real-time edits, significantly speeding up the debugging process.

Cincom VisualWorks: This offering from Cincom Systems is one of the most comprehensive commercial Smalltalk environments available today. VisualWorks is renowned for its scalability, portability, and rich set of enterprise-grade features.

- **Integrated Development Environment:** VisualWorks provides a highly configurable environment tailored for both beginner and advanced Smalltalk developers.
- **Cross-platform Support:** This tool allows developers to create applications that are portable across several major operating systems including Windows, macOS, and Linux.

GemStone/S: While not an IDE in the traditional sense, GemStone/S provides a robust Smalltalk-based persistent object database and a platform for developing, deploying, and managing scalable, multi-user applications. It introduces the dimension of data persistence and robust transaction management to Smalltalk applications.

- **Scalability:** It excels in scenarios where application scalability is crucial, managing large datasets efficiently.

- **Integration:** GemStone/S can integrate with other development tools, bringing persistent data management capabilities to Smalltalk environments.

Dolphin Smalltalk: Exclusive to Windows, Dolphin Smalltalk stands out for its rich graphical development environment and comprehensive library of widgets, making it particularly suited for desktop application development.

- **User Interface Development:** Dolphin excels in offering tools for building sophisticated user interfaces with a low learning curve.

- **Active Community:** Despite its platform limitation, Dolphin benefits from a dedicated and resourceful community, providing a wealth of third-party libraries and tools.

Each Smalltalk IDE and tool offers unique features that cater to different aspects of software development. Selecting the right environment depends on the project requirements, the target platform, and personal preference in development workflow. However, regardless of the choice, the integrated, and dynamic nature of Smalltalk IDEs guarantees a productive and enjoyable software development experience.

1.9 Setting Up a Smalltalk Development Environment

Setting up a development environment for Smalltalk is a critical first step in beginning your journey with this programming language. It involves selecting a suitable Integrated Development Environment (IDE) or programming environment, installing it on your system, and configuring it to suit your development needs. This process varies slightly depending on the specific Smalltalk implementation you choose to work with, as there are multiple, such as Squeak, Pharo, and VisualWorks, each with its unique features and installation procedures. This section will guide you through the general steps required to get a Smalltalk development environment up and running on your computer.

Selecting a Smalltalk Implementation

Several implementations of Smalltalk are available, each offering different features, libraries, and development tools. Some of the most popular include:

- **Squeak:** Known for its rich multimedia capabilities and educational tools.
- **Pharo:** Focuses on modern software development needs and has a vibrant community.
- **VisualWorks:** Offers a comprehensive development package for professional use.

Your choice should depend on your specific needs and the projects you intend to develop. For beginners, Pharo is often recommended due to its active community and extensive documentation.

Installation Process

Installing Pharo:

To install Pharo on your system, follow these steps:

1. Visit the Pharo official website and navigate to the download section.
2. Select the version of Pharo suitable for your operating system (Windows, macOS, or Linux).
3. Download the Pharo Launcher, which is a tool that allows you to manage multiple Pharo images (versions) easily.
4. Once downloaded, execute the installer or unzip the package, depending on the format provided for your OS.
5. Follow the on-screen instructions to complete the installation of the Pharo Launcher.

After installation, you can launch the Pharo Launcher to create and manage Pharo images. To create a new image:

1. Open the Pharo Launcher and click on the "New" button.
2. Choose a template for the Pharo version you wish to use and provide a name for your new image.
3. Click "Create" and wait for the process to complete. Once done, you can launch your newly created Pharo image.

Configuring Your Development Environment

Once you have installed and opened your selected Smalltalk environment, it is essential to familiarize yourself with the IDE's layout and features. Configuration options vary by implementation, but here are some general tips:

- Explore the settings or preferences menu to customize the look and feel of the environment.

- Familiarize yourself with the browser, workspace, transcript, and inspector windows, as these will be your primary tools for development in Smalltalk.
- Check for available packages or libraries that can be installed to extend the functionality of your environment.

For specific configurations related to development tasks like debugging, testing, and version control, refer to the documentation provided with your chosen Smalltalk implementation.

First Steps with Smalltalk

To get started with writing Smalltalk code, let's create a simple program that prints "Hello, World!" to the console. This will illustrate how to use the workspace and understand the syntax for message passing in Smalltalk.

```
"Print Hello, World to the Transcript"
Transcript show: 'Hello, World!'.
```

To execute this code:

1. Open the workspace window in your Smalltalk environment.
2. Copy and paste the code snippet above into the workspace.
3. Select the code and perform a do-it operation, which is usually executed by right-clicking and selecting the appropriate option or using a shortcut key, depending on your environment.

You should see "Hello, World!" printed in the Transcript window, which acts as a console output in many Smalltalk environments.

Setting up a Smalltalk development environment involves selecting a suitable implementation based on your project needs, installing it, and familiarizing yourself with the IDE's features and configurations. By following the detailed steps provided in this section for installation, configuration, and your first programming steps, you should now have a functional Smalltalk development environment ready for use in your projects.

1.10 Your First Smalltalk Program

Let's embark on the practical journey of Smalltalk programming by writing your first Smalltalk program. This will not only familiarize you with the programming environment but also give you hands-on experience with the language's syntax and its way of doing things. For our first program, we will start with something simple: a program that prints "Hello, Smalltalk!" to the console.

Setting Up the Environment

Before diving into the code, ensure that your Smalltalk development environment is properly set up. This entails having a Smalltalk IDE, like Pharo or Squeak, installed on your computer. If you haven't installed it yet, refer back to the "Setting Up a Smalltalk Development Environment" section for detailed instructions.

Writing the Code

Once your environment is ready, open your Smalltalk IDE and follow these steps:

1. Create a new workspace. This is usually done through the IDE's File menu.

2. In the workspace window, type the following code:

```
Transcript show: 'Hello, Smalltalk!'; cr.
```

3. Highlight the code you just typed.

4. Execute the code. This is typically done by right-clicking the highlighted code and selecting "Do it" or pressing a specific function key, depending on your IDE.

Understanding the Code

Let's dissect the code line you just wrote to understand what's happening:

- The `Transcript` object is a global object in Smalltalk used for output operations, similar to the console in other programming languages.

- `show: 'Hello, Smalltalk!'` sends a message to the `Transcript` object. In Smalltalk, sending a message is analogous to calling a method in other programming languages. This particular message instructs the `Transcript` to display the string "Hello, Smalltalk!".

- `cr` is another message sent to the `Transcript` object, asking it to move the cursor to the next line. This ensures that if any more text is displayed, it starts from a new line.

Running and Viewing the Output

After executing the code, look for the Transcript window in your IDE. You should see the output of the program there. If everything went according to plan, the output should be:

```
Hello, Smalltalk!
```

Congratulations! You've just written and executed your first Smalltalk program. Although simple, this program introduced you to the Smalltalk programming environment, the basic syntax, and how to run Smalltalk code. It is these foundational skills that you will build upon as you continue to explore more complex aspects of the language.

1.11 Exploring the Smalltalk Community and Resources

Engaging with the Smalltalk community and utilizing available resources significantly enhances the learning and development process. Smalltalk, with its rich history and pivotal role in the evolution of object-oriented programming, boasts a vibrant and supportive community. This section delves into the various avenues through which one can connect with this community and access a wealth of resources.

Online Forums and Discussion Groups

Online forums and discussion groups are invaluable for getting answers to specific questions, sharing experiences, and staying updated on the latest trends in Smalltalk development. Here are some of the most notable platforms:

- The Smalltalk Reddit (`r/smalltalk`): A space for both beginners and experienced developers to discuss all things Smalltalk.
- Stack Overflow: While not Smalltalk-specific, many Smalltalk developers actively participate and provide solutions to programming challenges.
- The Squeak Dev mailing list: Ideal for those working with the Squeak implementation of Smalltalk, offering insights into Squeak-specific development issues.

Conferences and Meetups

Participating in conferences and meetups offers an unparalleled opportunity to learn from seasoned experts and network with fellow developers. Some of the key gatherings include:

- ESUG (European Smalltalk User Group) Conference: An annual event that rotates through cities in Europe, showcasing workshops, talks, and sprints.
- STIC (Smalltalk Industry Conference): Held in North America, this conference features presentations from various sectors of the Smalltalk community.
- Local Smalltalk-related meetups: Many cities around the world host regular meetups for Smalltalk enthusiasts. Platforms like Meetup.com can help locate these gatherings.

Learning Resources and Documentation

A variety of learning resources are available that cater to both beginners and experienced programmers seeking to deepen their Smalltalk knowledge. These include:

- Official documentation: Most Smalltalk distributions come with comprehensive documentation. For example, the Pharo Smalltalk distribution offers extensive guides and tutorials.
- Online tutorials and courses: Websites like Udemy, Coursera, and edX occasionally offer courses on Smalltalk programming.
- Books: Several classic texts serve as excellent resources for learning Smalltalk, such as "Smalltalk-80: The Language and Its Implementation" and "Smalltalk by Example: the Developer's Guide".

Open Source Projects and Libraries

Engaging with open-source projects and libraries can accelerate the learning process by providing practical experience. Platforms such as GitHub host a multitude of Smalltalk projects, offering a chance to contribute to real-world applications. Not only does this enhance programming skills, but it also enriches one's portfolio.

The Smalltalk community and resources provide a robust support system for both novices and experienced developers. By leveraging online platforms, engaging in community events, utilizing learning materials, and participating in open-source projects, individuals can significantly enhance their Smalltalk proficiency and contribute to the growth of this enduring programming language.

Chapter 2

Understanding Smalltalk Syntax

Grasping the syntax of Smalltalk is crucial for developing fluency in this object-oriented programming language. Characterized by its simplicity and readability, Smalltalk's syntax deviates from many traditional programming languages, offering a unique approach that leverages messaging among objects. This chapter delves into the intricacies of Smalltalk's syntax, presenting an overview of its basic structure, variables, message passing mechanisms, and control structures. By dissecting these core components, readers will acquire the foundational knowledge necessary to craft efficient Smalltalk programs and harness the full potential of object-oriented programming in Smalltalk.

2.1 Basic Syntax Overview

Let's start with the foundation of any language: its syntax. In Smalltalk, the syntax is not only a set of rules for structuring code but also a philosophy of simplicity and directness that guides the interaction between objects. Due to its highly readable nature, Smalltalk code closely resembles natural language, which sets it apart from more symbol-heavy languages.

- **Statements:** Every instruction or statement in Smalltalk ends with a period (`.`). This mirrors the end of a sentence in natural language, clearly demarcating the conclusion of an operation or command.

- **Messages:** At the heart of Smalltalk syntax is the concept of sending messages to objects. Messages can be unary (no arguments), binary (one argument), or keyword messages (one or more arguments). The structure of a message send is object-orientated, aligning with the form `receiver messageName`.

- **Blocks:** Encapsulated sets of instructions or code blocks are delimited by square brackets (`[ ]`). Blocks can be used as arguments in message sends, enabling powerful constructs like loops and conditionals.

- **Assignment:** The assignment operator in Smalltalk is `:=`. This symbol is used to assign a value to a variable. For example, `myVar := 5.`.

- **Comments:** Comments in Smalltalk are enclosed within double quotes (`" "`). This allows developers to include human-readable notes or explanations that do not affect code execution.

Let's observe a simple example that illustrates the use of statements, message sends, blocks, and comments in Smalltalk syntax.

```
"Assign the number 10 to a variable"
myNumber := 10.

"Send a message to myNumber asking for its square root"
result := myNumber sqrt.

"Print the result on the Transcript"
Transcript show: result.
```

The output of the above code, assuming successful execution, would be:

```
3.16227766016838
```

This output is the square root of 10, demonstrating how the combination of simple syntax elements - including message passing, assignment, and the use of the Transcript for output - allows for clear and straightforward expression of computational logic.

In summary, the foundational syntax of Smalltalk emphasizes readability and simplicity, with a common set of elements like statements, message sends, blocks, assignments, and comments enabling expressive and flexible code. By mastering these syntax basics, one can fluently navigate the more complex landscapes of object-oriented programming within the Smalltalk environment.

2.2 Variables and Constants

In Smalltalk programming, understanding the distinction between variables and constants is fundamental. Unlike many programming languages where variables and constants might be introduced with specific keywords or syntax, Smalltalk treats both with an elegance that is both simple and consistent with its object-oriented nature.

Variables in Smalltalk

Variables in Smalltalk are placeholders or references to objects. The language does not classify variables by their data type, rather by the role they play or the scope in which they are declared. Smalltalk categorizes variables into three main types:

- Instance Variables: These are tied to a specific instance of a class. Each object instantiated from a class has its own set of instance variables.

- Class Variables: Unlike instance variables, class variables are shared across all instances of a class. They are used to store data relevant to the class as a whole, not to individual objects.

- Temporary Variables: These exist within a limited scope, typically within a method. They are used for storing temporary values needed during the execution of a method.

Declaration of these variables does not require a special syntax; it is done in the context of their usage. However, the convention dictates that variable names start with a lowercase letter and follow the camelCase notation.

An example to declare a temporary variable inside a method:

```
| tempVariable |
tempVariable := 10.
```

This snippet declares a temporary variable named `tempVariable` and assigns it the value 10.

Constants in Smalltalk

Smalltalk manages constants slightly differently. It does not have a dedicated syntax for declaring constants. However, the convention is to use class variables with names in all uppercase letters to signify constants. It's important to exercise discipline not to change the value of these "constants" as Smalltalk's dynamic nature allows it.

Example of defining a constant:

```
ClassName class>>initialize
    "Class initialization method"
    CONSTANTVALUE := 100.
```

Here, a class variable `CONSTANTVALUE` is intended to act as a constant, with its value set to 100. This value should not be changed during program execution.

Variable Assignment and Immutable Objects

In Smalltalk, variable assignment is accomplished using the := operator. This operator does not modify the object to which the variable currently refers; instead, it rebinds the variable to a new object. This distinction is crucial when working with immutable objects like Smalltalk's `String` and `Symbol`.

For example, assigning a new value to a variable:

```
myVar := 'Hello, World!'.
myVar := myVar, ' Goodbye!'.
```

In this example, `myVar` is initially bound to a string containing "Hello, World!". The next line concatenates " Goodbye!" to the current value of `myVar` and rebinds `myVar` to this new string. It is vital to understand that the original string is not altered; a new string is created and assigned back to `myVar`.

Understanding the nuances of variables and constants in Smalltalk is pivotal in mastering the language. The flexible yet disciplined approach offered by Smalltalk necessitates a deep comprehension of how objects are referenced and manipulated. Through deliberate practice and application of these concepts, developers can fully leverage the power of Smalltalk's object-oriented paradigm.

2.3 Messages: Syntax and Types

In Smalltalk, the concept of passing messages between objects is foundational and distinguishes it from other programming languages. Unlike traditional procedure calls, Smalltalk's message sending mechanism mimics real-world communication, where a message (or request) is sent to an object, and based on the message, the object performs an action or responds accordingly. This section will explore the syntax for message passing and dissect the types of messages Smalltalk supports: unary, binary, and keyword messages.

Message Passing Syntax

The general syntax for sending a message to an object is as follows:

```
receiver messageName
```

Here, the `receiver` is the object to which the message is sent, and `messageName` is the name of the message, specifying the action the receiver should take. Depending on the type of message, additional syntax rules apply.

Unary Messages

Unary messages are the simplest form of messages in Smalltalk. They consist of a single word and do not require any arguments. Unary messages are typically used to retrieve the value of an object or to perform an action that does not need supplementary data.

For example, sending a unary message to an object to obtain its size:

```
anArray size.
```

This message asks the array named `anArray` to return its size.

Binary Messages

Binary messages involve two participants: the receiver and a single argument. These messages are usually symbolic and are employed for performing arithmetic and logical operations.

For instance, adding two numbers together:

```
5 + 10.
```

Here, the message '+' is sent to the object `5` with `10` as its argument.

Keyword Messages

Keyword messages are the most expressive among Smalltalk messages, allowing the passing of multiple arguments by naming them within the message itself. This approach enhances readability and makes the code self-documenting to a large extent. The syntax includes keywords ending in a colon (:), each followed by an argument.

For example, to sort a collection by specifying the sort criteria:

```
aCollection sort: aBlock ascending: true.
```

In this case, `sort:` and `ascending:` are the keywords, with `aBlock` and `true` being their respective arguments. This message instructs `aCollection` to sort itself based on the criteria defined in `aBlock` and to perform the sort in ascending order.

Understanding Message Precedence

In Smalltalk, the order of execution for messages is determined by their type. Unary messages have the highest precedence, followed by binary messages, and finally, keyword messages have the lowest precedence. However, parentheses can be used to alter the default precedence, ensuring that messages inside the parentheses are executed first.

Consider the following example:

```
aNumber + 2 * 3.
```

Here, the binary message '*' is evaluated before '+' due to message precedence rules. However, to change the order of operations, you can use parentheses:

```
(aNumber + 2) * 3.
```

In this revised version, the addition is performed first, followed by the multiplication.

This section has elucidated the syntax and variations of messages in

Smalltalk. By understanding how to effectively compose and send messages, developers can leverage Smalltalk's powerful object-oriented capabilities to create dynamic and responsive applications.

2.4 Control Structures: Conditional and Loops

Control structures in Smalltalk, including conditional executions and loops, are fundamental in directing the flow of a program's execution. These structures allow developers to make decisions in their code and execute repetitive tasks efficiently. In this section, we will explore the syntax and usage of Smalltalk's control structures.

Conditional Execution

Conditional execution in Smalltalk is achieved through the use of `ifTrue:`, `ifFalse:`, `ifTrue:ifFalse:`, and `ifFalse:ifTrue:` messages that can be sent to Boolean objects. Unlike traditional `if-else` constructs found in languages like C or Java, Smalltalk uses these messages to perform actions based on conditions.

Here is a basic example of conditional execution:

```
(true) ifTrue: [ Transcript show: 'This will print.' ].
(false) ifFalse: [ Transcript show: 'This will also print.' ].
```

Moreover, Smalltalk allows for more complex conditional logic by nesting these messages:

```
(true) ifTrue: [
   Transcript show: 'This executes first.'
] ifFalse: [
   Transcript show: 'This will not execute.'
].
```

Loops

Loops in Smalltalk are implemented with messages that promote readability and clarity. The primary looping constructs are `whileTrue:`, `whileFalse:`, `to:do:`, and the `do:` message sent to collections.

While Loops

Using `whileTrue:` and `whileFalse:`, Smalltalk can perform a block of code repeatedly based on a condition. The following example demonstrates a simple counter implemented with a `whileTrue:` loop:

```
| counter |
counter := 0.
[ counter < 5 ] whileTrue: [
  Transcript show: 'Counter is at: ', counter printString; cr.
  counter := counter + 1.
].
```

For Loops

Smalltalk's equivalent of a for loop is achieved through the `to:do:` message, which iterates over a range of numbers. Here is an example:

```
1 to: 5 do: [ :index |
  Transcript show: 'Index is now: ', index printString; cr.
].
```

Iteration over Collections

Collections in Smalltalk can be easily iterated over using the `do:` message. This allows for each element in the collection to be accessed in sequence:

```
#('apple' 'banana' 'cherry') do: [ :fruit |
  Transcript show: 'Fruit: ', fruit; cr.
].
```

Conditional Loops

Additionally, Smalltalk provides a way to combine conditions and iteration in a single construct through conditional loops. For example, a `whileTrue:` loop can be used within a conditional execution block to perform complex loop operations based on certain conditions.

Understanding and applying Smalltalk's control structures—conditionals and loops—is crucial for creating robust and dynamic applications. By leveraging the readability and expressiveness of Smalltalk's syntax, developers can implement complex logic with concise and clear code. The provided examples offer a glimpse into the power and simplicity of programming in Smalltalk, paving the way for further exploration and mastery of this elegant language.

2.5 Understanding Methods: Definition and Invocation

Methods in Smalltalk are the building blocks for encapsulating functionality within objects. Every action that an object can perform is encapsulated within a method. Understanding how to define and invoke methods is fundamental to programming in Smalltalk. This section will guide the reader through the process of method definition, method invocation, and the nuances involved in these operations.

Methods in Smalltalk are defined within classes. Each method has a unique name within its class and can be identified by this name when being invoked. A method definition specifies the sequence of expressions that are executed when the method is invoked. Let's start with the syntactic structure used to define a method in Smalltalk.

```
methodName
    "Method comment"
    | localVariables |
    statements.
```

The method name, `methodName`, starts in the first column, followed by the method body. The method body can optionally start with a comment enclosed in double quotes. Local variables are declared between vertical bars and are only visible within the method. The executable part of the method consists of Smalltalk expressions, referred to here as `statements`, which are executed sequentially when the method is called.

A distinctive feature of Smalltalk is its use of messages to invoke methods. A message is sent to an object, which in turn looks for a method with a matching name in its class definition. If found, the method is executed; otherwise, a message-not-understood error is raised. There are three types of messages: unary, binary, and keyword messages, differing in syntax and the number of arguments they carry.

- Unary messages do not take any arguments and are used to access or modify the state of an object. Syntax example: `anObject size.`
- Binary messages take one argument and are usually used for arithmetic operations or comparison. Syntax example: `5 + 3.`
- Keyword messages take one or more arguments and are identified by keywords ending with colons. Syntax example: `anObject at: 1 put: 'a'.`

When invoking a method, the message is constructed according to the type of operation being performed and the number of arguments required. Below shows a simple method invocation using a unary message, assuming `anObject` is an instance of some class implementing a method named `size`.

```
anObject size.
```

The above sends a `size` message to `anObject`. If `anObject` has a `size` method defined in its class, that method is executed.

Below demonstrates invoking a method with a keyword message, which updates a certain position in a collection to a new value.

```
myCollection at: 1 put: 'a'.
```

This sends an `at:put:` message to the `myCollection` object with two arguments, `1` and `'a'`, respectively. The method corresponding to `at:put:` in `myCollection`'s class definition is then executed.

Adhering to the principles laid out in this section facilitates a deeper understanding of how methods function within the Smalltalk environment. Accurate method definition and invocation are pivotal in leveraging Smalltalk's message-passing paradigm to orchestrate complex behaviors in software systems.

2.6 Creating and Using Classes

In Smalltalk, a class is a blueprint from which objects are instantiated. Each class defines the properties (variables) and behaviors (methods) that its instances will have. This section will discuss the syntax for defining classes, creating instances, and understanding the role of the class in object-oriented programming within Smalltalk.

Class Definition

A class in Smalltalk is defined using the Smalltalk class definition syntax. A basic class definition includes the class name, instance variables, and methods. Classes are usually defined inside the System Browser, a GUI tool for code development in Smalltalk environments. The syntax to define a new class named `MyClass` would be:

```
Object subclass: #MyClass
    instanceVariableNames: 'variable1 variable2'
    classVariableNames: ''
    poolDictionaries: ''
    category: 'MyCategory'
```

This code snippet creates a new class called `MyClass` that is a subclass of `Object`. It has two instance variables: `variable1` and `variable2`. The class belongs to a category named `MyCategory`, which helps in organizing the code.

Creating Instances

Once a class is defined, you can create instances (objects) of that class using the `new` message. The instantiation process allocates memory for the new object and initializes its instance variables. Below is an example of creating an instance of `MyClass`:

```
| myObject |
myObject := MyClass new.
```

The variable `myObject` now holds a reference to an instance of `MyClass`.

Initializing Objects

It is often necessary to initialize an object's state immediately upon creation. Smalltalk uses the `initialize` method for this purpose, which is executed after an instance is created. By overriding the `initialize` method in your class, you can set the initial state of each instance:

```
MyClass>>initialize
    super initialize.
    variable1 := 1.
    variable2 := 2.
```

Ensure to call `super initialize` to execute the initialization code of the superclass before setting the instance variables.

Adding Methods to Classes

Methods in Smalltalk encapsulate the behavior that objects of the class exhibit. They are defined within the class definition using a similar syntax as for variable declaration but focus on behavior instead. For example, to add a method named `sum` that calculates the sum of `variable1` and `variable2`, you would write:

```
MyClass>>sum
    ^variable1 + variable2
```

The >> operator is used to indicate that the `sum` method belongs to `MyClass`. The^ character is used to return the result from the method.

Using Classes and Objects

With the class defined and instances created, you can invoke methods on the objects:

```
| myObject result |
myObject := MyClass new.
result := myObject sum.
```

This snippet creates a new instance of `MyClass` and assigns it to `myObject`. Then, it calls the `sum` method on `myObject` and stores the result in `result`.

In summary, classes in Smalltalk are defined with a series of descriptors for instance variables and methods. Instances of these classes are created with the `new` keyword, and their state can be initialized through the `initialize` method. Methods added to the class encapsulate the behavior of its instances, which can be invoked to perform operations or calculations. By mastering class creation and utilization, you lay the foundation for effective object-oriented programming in Smalltalk.

2.7 Inheritance: Syntax and Application

Inheritance is a cardinal concept in Smalltalk and foundational to its object-oriented design. It allows new classes to adopt the properties and behavior of existing classes, facilitating code reuse and the creation of a hierarchical class structure. By understanding inheritance, developers can extend the functionality of existing classes without modifying them directly, leading to more modular and maintainable code.

Defining a Subclass

In Smalltalk, a subclass inherits from a superclass. The syntax to define a subclass involves the \subclass: keyword within the class definition. Here is the general structure:

```
SuperclassName subclass: #NewClassName
    instanceVariableNames: 'variableNames'
    classVariableNames: 'classVariableNames'
    poolDictionaries: ''
    category: 'MyCategory'
```

In this template:

- SuperclassName is the name of the parent class from which properties and methods are inherited.
- #NewClassName is the name of the new class being defined. The hash sign (#) signifies that this is a symbol, a unique and immutable string in Smalltalk.
- instanceVariableNames and classVariableNames are strings that declare the names of the instance and class variables, respectively. These names are separated by spaces within the string.
- category is a string that specifies the grouping of the class within the Smalltalk environment, aiding in organization and retrieval.

Inheriting and Overriding Methods

When a class inherits from a superclass, it gains access to all its public methods. These methods can then be invoked on instances of the subclass. However, a subclass can also override these methods to provide specialized behavior. To override a method, simply define a method with the same name in the subclass.

```
NewClassName>>aMethod
    "method implementation"
```

This syntax indicates that aMethod, which was inherited from the superclass, is being redefined in NewClassName. It's important to use the override feature judiciously to prevent unintended behavior changes.

The super Keyword

Within overridden methods, the subclass can invoke the superclass's version of the method using the super keyword. This is particularly useful when extending rather than replacing the inherited method's behavior.

```
NewClassName>>aMethod
    super aMethod.
    "additional implementation"
```

Here, super aMethod calls the superclass's implementation of aMethod before executing the subclass's additional code.

Application of Inheritance

Leveraging inheritance effectively reduces duplication and increases the modularity of code. It allows for the creation of a more structured and hierarchical object model where common functionality is centralized in a superclass. Subclasses can then extend or specialize this functionality as needed.

For instance, consider a graphical application where various shapes have shared attributes such as color and position. By defining these properties in a superclass named Shape, subclasses like Circle, Rectangle, and Triangle can inherit these attributes. Each subclass may then define additional attributes and methods relevant to its specific shape, such as radius for a circle or sides and angles for a triangle.

```
Shape subclass: #Circle
    instanceVariableNames: 'radius'
    classVariableNames: ''
    poolDictionaries: ''
    category: 'Shapes'

```

```
Circle>>area
    "Calculates and returns the area of the circle."
    ^self radius squared * Float pi.
```

This example illustrates how inheritance in Smalltalk enables the creation of an organized and scalable system architecture, significantly enhancing the development of complex applications.

2.8 Polymorphism in Smalltalk

Polymorphism, one of the core concepts in object-oriented programming, allows objects of different classes to respond to the same message (or method call) in their unique manner. Smalltalk, with its pure object-oriented nature, provides a vivid environment to leverage polymorphism, enabling more flexible and reusable code.

In Smalltalk, polymorphism is inherently supported through its dynamic typing and late binding features. This means that the type of a variable is determined at runtime, and the exact code that gets executed when a message is sent to an object is also determined at runtime, based on the object's class.

Demonstration of Polymorphism

To illustrate polymorphism in Smalltalk, consider a scenario involving a collection of geometric shapes. Suppose we have a superclass named `Shape` with subclasses `Circle`, `Rectangle`, and `Triangle`. Each subclass has its own implementation of the method `calculateArea`. The polymorphism allows us to write code that can handle objects of any `Shape` subclass without knowing the specific type of shape at compile time.

```
Shape subclass: #Circle
    instanceVariableNames: 'radius'.
Circle methodsFor: 'calculating'
    calculateArea
        ^3.14 * radius * radius.

```

```
Shape subclass: #Rectangle
    instanceVariableNames: 'length width'.
Rectangle methodsFor: 'calculating'
    calculateArea
        ^length * width.

Shape subclass: #Triangle
    instanceVariableNames: 'base height'.
Triangle methodsFor: 'calculating'
    calculateArea
        ^(base * height) / 2.
```

Now, consider a function that accepts an object of type `Shape` and sends the `calculateArea` message to it:

```
calculateAreaFor: aShape
    ^aShape calculateArea.
```

Regardless of the shape type, the appropriate `calculateArea` method is invoked:

```
| circle rectangle triangle |
circle := Circle new.
circle radius: 5.
rectangle := Rectangle new.
rectangle length: 10; width: 20.
triangle := Triangle new.
triangle base: 5; height: 10.

{circle. rectangle. triangle} do: [:eachShape |
    Transcript show: eachShape calculateArea; cr].
```

Benefits of Polymorphism in Smalltalk

- **Code Reusability:** Polymorphism allows the same code to work with objects of different types, increasing code reusability and reducing redundancy.
- **Flexibility:** It offers flexibility in program design, as objects can be treated more abstractly, without specifying their exact types.
- **Ease of Maintenance:** Enhances the maintainability of code by isolating changes to specific subclasses, thus minimizing impact on existing code base.

Polymorphism in Smalltalk is realized through its dynamic type system and late binding mechanism, which allows objects to be treated abstractly. By doing so, Smalltalk enables the development of flexible, reusable, and maintainable software, fully exploiting the benefits of object-oriented programming. Understanding and applying polymorphism effectively can significantly enhance the quality and capability of Smalltalk programs.

2.9 Categorizing Methods and Protocols

In Smalltalk, the organization of methods into categories and protocols plays a significant role in enhancing code readability and maintainability. Unlike many programming languages where methods are typically grouped within the class definition, Smalltalk provides a more flexible approach that aids in navigating the codebase and understanding the functionality at a glance.

Methods

Methods in Smalltalk are essentially blocks of code associated with a particular class or instance that perform specific operations. Categorizing these methods logically is crucial for the effective management of code, especially in large projects. Here's how methods can be categorized:

- **Accessor Methods**: These methods are used to access the values of an object's instance variables. Typically, there are two types of accessor methods: getters and setters. For example, a method named `age` would return the age of an object, while `age:` would set the age.
- **Utility Methods**: Smalltalk programmers often encapsulate frequently used code blocks as utility methods. These methods perform general-purpose tasks and can be invoked by various objects.

- **Initialization and Cleanup**: Methods that prepare an object for use (initialization) or perform cleanup actions before an object is destroyed are categorized under this section.
- **Business Logic**: This category includes methods that perform the core functionalities related to the application's domain.

Protocols

Protocols in Smalltalk are akin to interfaces in other programming languages but are implemented as categories of methods without requiring explicit declarations. Protocols group methods that typically serve a common purpose or are logically related, aiding in the discovery of functionalities. Here are a few common protocols in Smalltalk:

- **Accessing**: Contains getter and setter methods, alongside other methods that provide direct access to an object's data.
- **Testing**: Groups methods used for condition checks, like `isEmpty` or `includes:`.
- **Enumerating**: Methods that facilitate iteration over a collection, such as `do:`, `collect:`, and `select:`.
- **Converting**: This protocol includes methods that convert an object from one type to another or to a different representation.

By adhering to a consistent method categorization and protocol definition, developers can vastly improve code navigation and interpretability. This structured approach not only aids in maintaining a clean codebase but also enhances collaboration among team members by setting clear expectations regarding method functionality and grouping.

For implementing these categorizations and protocols in your Smalltalk projects, consider the following code snippet:

```
Object subclass: #Person
   instanceVariableNames: 'name age'
   classVariableNames: ''
```

```
    poolDictionaries: ''
    category: 'Model'.

Person class >> age: anAge name: aName
    ^self new
        initializeAge: anAge;
        initializeName: aName;
        yourself.

Person >> initializeAge: anAge
    age := anAge.

Person >> initializeName: aName
    name := aName.

Person >> age
    ^age.

Person >> name
    ^name.
```

In the above example, the `Person` class is defined with instance variables `name` and `age` and methods categorized under appropriate protocols. The `initializeAge:` and `initializeName:` methods fall under an "initialization" category, while `age` and `name` are accessor methods.

Categorizing methods and adhering to established protocols streamlines the development process, making Smalltalk an exceptionally powerful tool for object-oriented programming. By embracing this structured approach, developers can create easily navigable, maintainable, and understandable codebases, thereby harnessing the full potential of Smalltalk's object-oriented capabilities.

2.10 Selectors and Blocks

Selectors in Smalltalk are unique identifiers that enable message passing between objects. A selector is essentially the name of the method that is being invoked on the receiver object. The power of selectors lies in their ability to be treated as first-class objects, allowing them to be stored in variables, passed as arguments, and dynamically invoked.

Let's start with an understanding of selectors. Consider the following example:

```
| anArray aSelector |
anArray := #('Smalltalk' 'is' 'powerful').
aSelector := #atRandom.
anArray perform: aSelector.
```

In the example above, `anArray` is an array object containing three strings. `aSelector` is a variable holding the selector `#atRandom`, which is a method available on collections that returns a random element. The `perform:` method is used on `anArray` to dynamically invoke the method corresponding to the selector stored in `aSelector`. The output of executing this snippet would be a random element from `anArray`, as shown here:

```
'Smalltalk'
```

This output is one possible result, reflecting the dynamic nature of message passing in Smalltalk.

Moving on to blocks, a block in Smalltalk is an enclosed segment of code that can be executed at a later time. Blocks can take arguments, can contain local variables, and can return a value. They are, in essence, anonymous functions or closures in other programming languages.

Here is an example demonstrating the usage of blocks:

```
| blockResult |
blockResult := [:x | x * x] value: 3.
Transcript show: blockResult printString.
```

In this snippet, a block is defined that takes one argument, `x`, and returns `x` squared. The block is immediately executed with `3` as the argument by sending it the message `value:`. The result is stored in `blockResult`, which would then equal 9. The output is as follows:

```
9
```

Blocks are a pivotal feature of Smalltalk that allows for sophisticated control structures, iteration, and event handling by delegating blocks of code as callbacks or handlers.

Lastly, it is important to grasp how both selectors and blocks are instrumental in Smalltalk's reflective capabilities and its highly dynamic and flexible message-passing system. They enable writing concise, expressive, and reusable code. Practicing with these constructs will greatly enhance fluency in Smalltalk programming.

2.11 Commenting Code and Best Practices

Commenting code is an integral part of programming in any language, including Smalltalk. Properly commented code is easier to read, understand, and maintain. In Smalltalk, comments play an especially crucial role due to the language's emphasis on readability and simplicity. This section elucidates the best practices for commenting code in Smalltalk, highlighting the importance of clarity and conciseness.

Smalltalk uses double quotes ("") to enclose comments in the code. Comments can be inserted almost anywhere within the code without affecting its execution. Here's an example:

```
"Initialize an instance of MyClass"
myInstance := MyClass new.
```

The comment above explains the purpose of the code line, making it clear to anyone reading the code what the intent was. This level of clarity is vital for maintenance and collaboration in coding projects.

Best Practices for Commenting Code

While commenting is crucial, over-commenting or under-commenting can lead to its own set of problems. Here are best practices to follow when commenting your Smalltalk code:

- **Use comments to explain the *why*, not the *how*.** The code itself should be clear enough to explain how it functions, but the reasoning behind certain decisions may not always be apparent. Use comments to provide this context.

- **Keep comments up-to-date**. Obsolete or misleading comments can be more harmful than no comments at all. Ensure that comments are updated or removed as the code evolves.
- **Avoid redundant comments**. Comments should not restate what is already obvious from the code. For example, avoid commenting on variable increments in a loop unless it has an unconventional purpose.
- **Use comments to divide the code into logical sections**. This can help readers navigate the code more easily, especially in lengthy methods or when using complex algorithms.
- **Document the function of each method and class at the beginning**. A brief comment about the purpose and usage of each method and class can significantly enhance the code's understandability.

An example of method documentation can be seen below:

```
"Method: addNumbers: aNumber anotherNumber: anotherNumber
Adds two numbers and returns the result."
addNumbers: aNumber anotherNumber: anotherNumber
    ^aNumber + anotherNumber.
```

In addition to inline comments and method documentation, Smalltalk provides mechanisms for categorizing methods and defining protocols, which serve as an indirect form of commenting. By organizing methods into categories related to their functionality, you inherently document the code structure, making it easier for others to follow.

Commenting for Debugging and Testing

Comments can also be a valuable tool during the debugging and testing phases. Temporary comments might include:

- **To-do items**, marking spots where additional work is needed or where a bug was discovered.

- **Debugging hints**, such as recommendations for future tests or conditions under which a bug occurs.

It is important, however, to clean up such temporary comments once they are no longer needed, to avoid clutter and confusion.

To conclude, in Smalltalk, as in any programming language, commenting is both an art and a discipline. Effective comments enhance the readability and maintainability of code, making it more accessible to others and facilitating collaboration. By adhering to the best practices outlined above, Smalltalk programmers can ensure their comments are both helpful and meaningful.

2.12 Common Syntax Pitfalls and How to Avoid Them

In this section, we will discuss common syntax pitfalls encountered by programmers when working with Smalltalk and strategies to avoid them. Awareness and understanding of these pitfalls can significantly enhance the efficiency and quality of your Smalltalk programming.

- **Omitting Periods between Statements**: In Smalltalk, periods (`.`) are used to separate statements. A common mistake is forgetting to place a period between two statements, which can lead to unexpected behavior or syntax errors.

  Consider the correct usage:

```
Smalltalk at: #Counter put: 0.
Counter := Counter + 1.
```

- **Incorrect Message Sending Syntax**: Remember that Smalltalk uses message passing as its primary mechanism for invoking behavior. The syntax for message sending must follow the pattern `[receiver] [messageName]` for unary messages, `[receiver] [messageName: argument]` for keyword messages, and `[receiver] [messageName] [argument]` for binary messages. Failure to adhere to this syntax can lead to syntax errors or unintended behavior.

- **Confusing Assignment with Equality Comparison**: Smalltalk uses := for variable assignments and = for equality comparison. Mixing up these operators can lead to subtle bugs. For example:

```
a := 5. "Correct usage for assignment"
b := a = 5. "b is assigned the result of the comparison"
```

- **Misusing Blocks**: Blocks in Smalltalk are powerful tools that encapsulate a set of instructions to be executed later. A common mistake is forgetting to invoke a block when its execution is required, or incorrectly passing arguments to it.

  To correctly invoke a block with no arguments:

```
[Transcript show: 'Hello, World!'] value.
```

- **Variable Shadowing in Nested Scopes**: Variable shadowing occurs when a variable declared within a certain scope has the same name as a variable outside that scope. This can lead to unexpected behavior, as the inner variable takes precedence over the outer one. Be mindful of naming variables to avoid shadowing, especially in nested blocks or method definitions.

- **Forgetting to Send `super` Messages in Overrides**: When overriding methods in subclasses, it is crucial to remember to send a `super` message to the parent class when its original implementation needs to be preserved or extended. Neglecting to send a `super` message can lead to incomplete or incorrect behavior of the subclass.

  Implementation of `super` message:

```
Animal >> walk
    "Parent class method"
    Transcript show: 'Animal is walking'.

Cat >> walk
    "Overridden method"
    super walk.
    Transcript show: '...gracefully'.
```

By familiarizing oneself with these common syntax pitfalls and their avoidance strategies, programmers can reduce the occurrence of errors and improve the readability and maintainability of their Smalltalk code. Each pitfall mentioned is accompanied by clear examples or corrective measures to ensure clarity and facilitate effective learning.

Chapter 3

Working with Smalltalk Classes and Methods

The concept of classes and methods forms the backbone of Smalltalk's object-oriented programming model, allowing for the encapsulation of data and behavior within reusable components. This chapter explores the creation and utilization of classes and methods in Smalltalk, from defining and instantiating classes to understanding the nuances of instance and class variables, inheritance, and polymorphism. By engaging with these fundamental aspects, readers will learn to design robust, modular software systems in Smalltalk, adhering to principles that ensure code reusability and clarity.

3.1 Introduction to Classes and Instances

Let's start with the foundational concepts of classes and instances in Smalltalk, which are essential for understanding object-oriented programming. In Smalltalk, everything is an object, and these objects are instances of classes. A class provides a blueprint for creating objects, defining the properties (attributes) and behaviors (methods) that its instances will have.

Consider a class as a template for an object. For instance, you might have a Person class that describes the characteristics and actions that a person can have. Each individual person is an object or instance of the Person class. These instances possess the characteristics and actions defined by the class.

To define a class in Smalltalk, one uses its class definition syntax. A simple class definition includes the class name, its superclass (from which it inherits attributes and methods), and its own unique attributes and methods. For example:

```
Object subclass: #Person
    instanceVariableNames: 'name age'
    classVariableNames: ''
    poolDictionaries: ''
    category: 'MyApplication'.
```

This code snippet creates a new class named Person, which is a subclass of Object, the root class of all classes in Smalltalk. The Person class has two instance variables, name and age, which are attributes that will be unique to each instance of the class.

Instances of a class are created by sending the class a message that invokes a constructor method. In Smalltalk, this is typically done with the new message. The newly created object is initially empty, and its instance variables are not set. After creating an object, one typically sends messages to it to initialize its state. For example, to create a new instance of Person and initialize its name and age, you would do:

```
| john |
john := Person new.
john name: 'John Doe'.
john age: 30.
```

This series of expressions assigns a new Person instance to the variable john. It then sends two messages, name: and age:, to john to set its name and age, respectively.

Understanding the distinction between classes and instances is crucial. A class defines the structure and behavior of objects, while an instance is an actual object created based on the class blueprint. The class holds the template for its instances: its variables describe what data the instances can hold, and its methods define what operations can be performed on this data.

In summary, classes and instances are the core components of the object-oriented paradigm in Smalltalk. Classes act as blueprints for creating objects (instances), which encapsulate both data (through instance variables) and behaviors (via methods). This design allows for modular, reusable code that is easy to maintain and extend.

3.2 Defining and Instantiating Classes

In Smalltalk, defining a class involves specifying its name, its superclass (from which it inherits behavior and properties), instance variables (which hold state information for each object), and class variables (shared across all instances of the class). The class definition also includes the methods that will operate on these variables, providing the object's behavior.

To define a class in Smalltalk, one typically uses the class browser, a tool within the Smalltalk environment. The basic syntax for class definition is straightforward and highly readable, reflecting the language's emphasis on readability and simplicity. Here is a hypothetical example of defining a class named `Person`:

```
Object subclass: #Person
    instanceVariableNames: 'name age'
    classVariableNames: ''
    poolDictionaries: ''
    category: 'MyApplication'
```

This code snippet defines a new class named `Person` that is a subclass of `Object`, indicating that it inherits from the root of the Smalltalk class hierarchy. The class `Person` has two instance variables, `name` and age, which are intended to hold the name and age of the person, respectively. The `classVariableNames` and `poolDictionaries` are left empty in this example, indicating that `Person` does not use these features. Finally, the class is placed in the category 'MyApplication', which helps organize the class within the Smalltalk environment's class library.

After defining a class, creating (or "instantiating") objects from the class is a matter of sending the `new` message to the class itself. The class responds to this message by creating a new instance of itself. Here is an example of instantiating a `Person` object:

```
| john |
john := Person new.
```

In this example, the variable `john` holds the reference to a new instance of `Person`. At this point, the instance variables `name` and `age` are uninitialized.

To initialize the `Person` object with specific data, one usually defines an initializer method within the class. For instance:

```
Person >> initializeWithName: aName age: anAge
    name := aName.
    age := anAge.
```

This method, `initializeWithName: age:`, is an instance method of the class `Person`, taking two arguments: a name and an age. It initializes the instance variables `name` and `age` of the `Person` instance. To use this initializer, one would send the `initializeWithName: age:` message to the newly created `Person` object:

```
john := Person new.
john initializeWithName: 'John Doe' age: 30.
```

The combination of class definition, object instantiation, and initialization through specialized methods form the basis of creating and working with objects in Smalltalk. By carefully defining classes and corresponding initializer methods, Smalltalk programmers can effectively encapsulate data and behavior within objects, making it possible to build complex, modular software systems.

This approach emphasizes clarity, reusability, and the principles of object-oriented programming, allowing Smalltalk developers to create sophisticated applications that are both maintainable and extensible.

3.3 Understanding Instance Variables and Methods

In this section we will discuss the foundation of creating dynamic, responsive objects within Smalltalk: the implementation and use of instance variables and methods. This critical component underpins the object-oriented nature of Smalltalk, enabling the encapsulation of state and behavior in an object.

Instance variables are the primary mechanism for an object to store its state. Unlike class variables, which are shared across all instances of a class, instance variables are unique to each object. When an object is created, Smalltalk allocates space in memory for each instance variable declared in the object's class definition.

The syntax for declaring instance variables in Smalltalk is straightforward. Within the class definition, instance variables are declared between vertical bars after the class name, as shown in the following example:

```
Object subclass: #Person
    instanceVariableNames: 'name age'
    classVariableNames: ''
    poolDictionaries: ''
    category: 'MyApplication'.
```

In this example, the `Person` class has two instance variables, `name` and `age`. These variables are private to each `Person` object and hold data specific to that object.

Moving to methods, they define the behavior of an object and are akin to functions or procedures in other programming languages. However, in Smalltalk, methods are always associated with an object — either an instance of a class or the class itself. Instance methods operate on the instance variables of the object, providing the functionality to inspect or modify the object's state. Methods are defined within the class definition, following the instance variable declaration.

To define a method in Smalltalk, the syntax includes the method name, arguments (if any), and a series of statements to be executed when the method is called. Methods can return a value using the ^ character. For example, a simple method to return the full name of a person might look like this:

```
fullName
    ^ name, ' ', age asString
```

This `fullName` method concatenates the `name` instance variable with the string representation of the `age` instance variable, separated by a space. The ^ character indicates that the result of this concatenation is the return value of the method.

Methods can also take arguments, which are passed between parentheses after the method name. For instance, to update a person's name, one might define the following method:

```
setName: aName
    name := aName.
```

This method, named `setName:`, assigns the value of its argument, `aName`, to the `name` instance variable of the object. It's worth noting that method names in Smalltalk can include colons; this is a convention indicating that the method expects an argument.

Instance variables and methods together form the essence of class definitions in Smalltalk. Instance variables hold the data unique to each object, while methods define how that data can be manipulated and interacted with. Understanding these concepts is fundamental to mastering object-oriented programming in Smalltalk, as they enable the creation of rich, dynamic classes that encapsulate both data and behavior.

3.4 Class Variables and Class Methods Explained

Class variables and class methods in Smalltalk are critical aspects that facilitate the sharing of data and behavior across all instances of a class, as well as provide functionalities pertinent to the class itself, rather than to any individual object instantiated from that class. This distinction plays a crucial role in the design and implementation of scalable and maintainable software systems.

Class Variables

Class variables in Smalltalk are shared across all instances of a class. Unlike instance variables, which are unique to each object, class variables maintain a single state that is accessible and mutable by every instance of the class, as well as by the class methods.

To define a class variable in Smalltalk, it is declared in the class definition area within a pair of parentheses. For instance:

```
Object subclass: #MyClass
    instanceVariableNames: ''
    classVariableNames: 'SharedCounter'
    poolDictionaries: ''
    category: 'MyCategory'.
```

In this example, `MyClass` declares a class variable named `SharedCounter`. This variable is accessible to all instances of `MyClass` and can be used to perform operations that need a shared state among instances.

Accessing Class Variables

Class variables can be accessed and mutated using class methods or instance methods. To access or mutate a class variable's value, you typically define accessor and mutator methods at the class level. For example:

```
MyClass class >> sharedCounter
    ^SharedCounter
```

```
MyClass class >> incrementSharedCounter
    SharedCounter := SharedCounter + 1.
```

In these examples, the first method provides read access to the `SharedCounter` class variable, while the second method increments its value. Notice the syntax: the class methods are defined with the class keyword following the class name.

Class Methods

Class methods in Smalltalk are associated with the class itself rather than with instances of the class. They can be used to implement functionality relevant to the class as a whole such as factory methods, which are methods designed to instantiate and return objects of a class.

Definition of a class method is straightforward. For example, to define a class method that returns a new instance of MyClass with a predefined state:

```
MyClass class >> withDefaultState
    ^self new initializeWithDefaultState.
```

This method, withDefaultState, can be invoked directly on the class object to obtain a new instance of MyClass in the default state. The self keyword in the context of a class method refers to the class itself, not to an instance of the class.

Importance of Class Methods and Variables

Class methods and variables serve multiple purposes in Smalltalk programming. They allow for the encapsulation of class-wide logic and data, facilitating a design that adheres to the DRY principle (Don't Repeat Yourself). By centralizing shared state and behavior at the class level, developers can reduce redundancy, enhance code clarity, and ensure that updates to the shared state are uniformly reflected across all instances of the class.

Understanding and applying class variables and class methods are foundational in creating robust and reusable Object-Oriented software with Smalltalk. By leveraging these constructs, developers can design their classes to encapsulate not only instance-specific behaviors and data but also those that are shared across instances, promoting a clean and modular architectural design.

3.5 Inheritance: Creating Subclasses

Inheritance is a fundamental concept in object-oriented programming, allowing for a hierarchy of classes where a child class inherits properties and methods from its parent class. In Smalltalk, this mechanism enables developers to create subclasses that encapsulate specific behaviors or attributes while sharing common features with their parent classes.

To implement inheritance in Smalltalk, the subclass specifies its parent class at the time of its definition. This is achieved using the `subclass:` method, where the subclass declares not only its inheritance from a parent class but also its instance variables. For example, to create a subclass named `Rectangle` that inherits from a superclass named `Shape`, the code snippet would be:

```
Rectangle subclass: Shape
    instanceVariableNames: 'width height'
    classVariableNames: ''
    poolDictionaries: ''
    category: 'Geometry'.
```

In this example, `Rectangle` adds two instance variables, `width` and `height`, which are specific to the `Rectangle` class but does not affect the `Shape` class. The `Rectangle` class inherits all of `Shape`'s instance variables and methods, which means any instance of `Rectangle` can utilize the inherited methods, in addition to the methods defined explicitly within the `Rectangle` class.

Understanding the Implications of Inheritance

Inheritance encourages code reuse by allowing classes to inherit functionality from their parent classes. This also fosters a logical and hierarchical organization of code, simplifying maintenance and understanding of the code base. Consider the following implications of inheritance in the design of a class hierarchy:

- **Reusability**: Subclasses reuse code from their parent classes, reducing duplication.

- **Extensibility**: It is easy to extend software by adding new subclasses which immediately inherit properties and behaviors from existing classes.
- **Maintainability**: Changes made to a parent class automatically propagate to subclasses, centralizing updates and minimizing errors.

Polymorphism and Inheritance

Polymorphism, another key concept in object-oriented programming, works hand-in-hand with inheritance. It allows a subclass instance to be treated as an instance of its parent class, enabling the same interface to serve different underlying data types. In Smalltalk, polymorphism manifests through method overriding, where a subclass redefines a method inherited from its parent class to perform a function that's specific to the subclass.

For instance, if both `Shape` and `Rectangle` classes have a method named `area`, the `Rectangle` class can override this method to compute the area of a rectangle specifically. When an `area` message is sent to a `Rectangle` object, Smalltalk's dynamic dispatcher ensures the overridden method in the `Rectangle` class is called:

```
Shape subclass: Rectangle
    instanceVariableNames: 'width height'
    classVariableNames: ''
    poolDictionaries: ''
    category: 'Geometry'.

Rectangle >> area
    ^ width * height.
```

Through inheritance and polymorphism, Smalltalk supports the development of flexible and robust systems. Classes can define their unique attributes and behaviors while leveraging the functionality provided by their ancestors, promoting code reusability and scalability.

Considering these principles, developers should design their class hierarchies carefully, promoting clear relationships and responsibilities among classes to maintain a clean and efficient codebase.

3.6 Method Overriding and Super Calls

Method overriding is a key concept in achieving polymorphism in object-oriented programming languages like Smalltalk. It allows a subclass to provide a specific implementation of a method that is already defined in its superclass. This section elucidates the mechanism of method overriding in Smalltalk and delves into the usage of super calls to invoke the implementation of a superclass method from a subclass method.

Understanding Method Overriding

In Smalltalk, when a subclass redefines a method that is already defined in one of its superclasses, it is said to "override" that method. This overriding mechanism is essential for polymorphism, allowing an object to exhibit different behaviors when a message corresponding to the overridden method is sent to it, depending on the object's class.

Consider an example where a class `Animal` has a method `makeSound`. A subclass `Dog` might override this method to provide a more specific implementation, like so:

```
Animal class>>makeSound
    ^'Some generic animal sound'.

Dog class>>makeSound
    ^'Bark'.
```

In this example, sending the message `makeSound` to an instance of `Animal` would return the string `'Some generic animal sound'`, while sending the same message to an instance of `Dog` would return `'Bark'`.

Super Calls

A subclass may sometimes want to not only provide its own implementation for a method but also leverage the implementation provided by its superclass. This is where super calls come into play. Using the keyword `super` in Smalltalk allows a subclass method to call its superclass's implementation of that method.

Revisiting the `Animal` and `Dog` classes, suppose we want the `Dog`'s `makeSound` method to include both the generic animal sound and the dog-specific sound. This can be achieved with a super call:

```
Dog class>>makeSound
    ^super makeSound, ' and Bark'.
```

The result of sending the `makeSound` message to an instance of `Dog` now would be the string `'Some generic animal sound and Bark'`.

Practical Considerations and Best Practices

When overriding methods and making super calls, there are several key considerations:

- Overriding should be used judiciously. While it is a powerful tool for polymorphism, indiscriminate overriding can make the code harder to understand and maintain.
- Super calls are best used when the subclass wants to extend rather than completely replace the behavior of a superclass method.
- It is important to ensure that super calls do not lead to infinite recursion. This can happen if the superclass method being called also makes a call to the subclass method.

To summarize, method overriding and super calls are fundamental to leveraging polymorphism and reusability in Smalltalk. They enable subclasses to modify or extend the behavior of methods defined in superclasses in a controlled and meaningful way.

3.7 Working with Constructors and Initializers

Constructors and initializers play a crucial role in the lifecycle of objects in Smalltalk. These constructs facilitate the setting up of an object's initial state, ensuring it is ready for use immediately after creation. Unlike in some other object-oriented languages, Smalltalk's approach to constructors and initializers is deeply rooted in its message-passing paradigm. This section elucidates the mechanisms for defining and using constructors and initializers in Smalltalk, focusing on their syntax, usage patterns, and best practices.

In Smalltalk, the standard mechanism for creating an object is to send the message `new` to a class. This message is understood by all classes and is inherited from the `Object` superclass. The `new` message triggers the execution of an instance creation method that allocates memory for a new instance of the class and returns it. By default, this operation does not initialize the instance variables of the new object; they are left in an undefined state. To equip an object with a meaningful initial state, Smalltalk provides initializers.

An initializer is a method that sets up an object's instance variables with appropriate initial values. It is a common practice to define an initializer method in the class of the object. An initializer is typically invoked immediately after an object is created. The naming convention for initializers is not enforced by the language but, by convention, initializers often begin with the word 'initialize'.

Let's illustrate this with an example of a class named `Person`, which has two instance variables `name` and `age`:

```
Person class>>newWithName: aName age: anAge
    ^self new initializeWithName: aName age: anAge
```

In the example above, the class method `newWithName:age:` is defined on the class side of `Person`. This method first sends the message `new` to `self` (which is `Person` class in this context), to create a new instance. Following this, it sends the instance a message `initializeWithName:age:` with the provided name and age as arguments. This pattern separates the concerns of creating an object (handled by `new`) and initializing an object (handled by `initializeWithName:age:`).

Here is how one might define the `initializeWithName:age:` method on the instance side:

```
initializeWithName: aName age: anAge
    name := aName.
    age := anAge.
```

This initializer method sets the instance variables `name` and `age` to the values passed as arguments.

After defining the constructor and initializer, creating and initializing a `Person` object can be done as follows:

```
| johnDoe |
johnDoe := Person newWithName: 'John Doe' age: 30.
```

The creation of `johnDoe` exemplifies the default approach in Smalltalk for constructing and initializing objects. It combines the power of custom class methods for object creation with the flexibility of instance methods for initialization, adhering closely to the principles of encapsulation and message passing.

Constructors and initializers in Smalltalk are instrumental in setting up objects. By following the outlined patterns of using `new` along with customized initializing methods, developers can ensure their objects start their lifecycle in a well-defined state, thus contributing to the robustness and clarity of the software system.

3.8 Understanding Accessor and Mutator Methods

Accessor and mutator methods, commonly referred to as getters and setters, play a central role in Object-Oriented Programming (OOP) by controlling access to an object's attributes. This section will elaborate on the purpose and implementation of accessor and mutator methods in Smalltalk, showcasing their utility in safeguarding the integrity of an object's data while also adhering to the principle of encapsulation.

In Smalltalk, accessor methods are used to retrieve or access the value of an object's instance variable. Conversely, mutator methods are used to set or modify the value of an object's instance variable. It is through these methods that Smalltalk achieves a high degree of data encapsulation, a fundamental OOP concept that restricts direct access to some of an object's components.

```
"Example of an accessor method for a 'Person' class"
Person >> name
    ^name

"Example of a mutator method for a 'Person' class"
Person >> name: anObject
    name := anObject
```

The preceding code illustrates the basic structure of accessor and mutator methods in Smalltalk for a simple `Person` class. The accessor method `name` simply returns the value of the instance variable `name`, whereas the mutator method `name:` takes an argument (`anObject`) and assigns its value to the `name` instance variable.

The use of accessor and mutator methods not only encapsulates the internal representation of an object but also offers a layer of abstraction. This means that the internal implementation of an object can later be modified without affecting the external code that depends on it. For instance, if the internal storage mechanism of the `name` attribute in the `Person` class changes, only the `name` and `name:` methods would need adjustment. The rest of the application remains unaffected, as long as it interacts with the `name` attribute via these methods.

Additionally, mutator methods can incorporate validation logic to ensure that only valid data is assigned to an object's instance variables. This enhances the robustness of a program by preventing the object from entering an inconsistent state.

```
"Enhanced mutator method with validation"
Person >> name: anObject
    (anObject isKindOf: String) ifTrue: [name := anObject] ifFalse: [self error:
         'Invalid name'].
```

In this enhanced mutator method example, the `name:` method first checks if the provided argument is a string. If it is not, an error is raised. This ensures that the `name` instance variable of the `Person` class can only be assigned a string value, maintaining the integrity of the object's data.

In summary, accessor and mutator methods serve as the gatekeepers to an object's data in Smalltalk, offering both protection and flexibility. By abstracting the way in which data is accessed and modified, these methods uphold the principles of encapsulation and data integrity, which are vital for building robust and maintainable software systems.

3.9 Method Overloading in Smalltalk

Method overloading, a concept widely recognized in many object-oriented programming languages, allows multiple methods within the same class to share the same name but differ in the number or type of parameters they accept. However, it's crucial to understand that Smalltalk, with its dynamic and highly flexible nature, does not support method overloading in the same manner as statically typed languages like Java or C++. Instead, Smalltalk adopts a different approach to achieve similar functionality, focusing on method overriding and the dynamic dispatch of methods.

In Smalltalk, every method is uniquely identified by its selector, which includes the method name and the sequence of colons (:) indicating the number of arguments. This means that what might appear to be method overloading in other languages is actually achieved through distinctly named methods in Smalltalk.

Consider the following example, which attempts to replicate the overloading functionality:

```
MyClass >> add: aNumber to: anotherNumber
    ^aNumber + anotherNumber.

MyClass >> add: aString to: anotherString
    ^aString, anotherString.
```

In the code snippet above, both methods are designed to 'add' elements, but their parameters differ in type—one accepts numbers, and the other strings. However, this is not method overloading, but rather two completely distinct methods that happen to share a common prefix in their selectors. Smalltalk's messaging system can distinguish between them thanks to their unique selectors.

To further illustrate the point that Smalltalk does not support traditional method overloading, consider the scenario where a developer attempts to define methods solely differentiated by parameter type:

```
MyClass >> addNumbers: aNumber anotherNumber: anotherNumber
    ^aNumber + anotherNumber.

MyClass >> addStrings: aString anotherString: anotherString
    ^aString, anotherString.
```

Here, the differentiation between the methods is made explicit through their selectors ('addNumbers:anotherNumber:' vs. 'addStrings:anotherString:'), ensuring clarity in method purpose and avoiding the ambiguities that traditional overloading might introduce.

Smalltalk's approach emphasizes clear and expressive method names, encouraging developers to think critically about method functionality and its interaction with objects. This design choice aligns with Smalltalk's philosophy of readability and simplicity, ensuring code is self-describing and easy to understand.

While method overloading as understood in statically typed languages is not present in Smalltalk, the language offers its own powerful mechanisms for handling diverse method functionality. By leveraging descriptive method names and embracing Smalltalk's dynamic typing system, developers can achieve similar outcomes without compromising on code clarity and maintainability. This paradigm encourages a thoughtful consideration of method design, reinforcing the principles of clean and effective object-oriented programming.

3.10 Using Categories for Organizing Methods

In this section, we will discuss the concept of using categories for organizing methods in Smalltalk. Categories in Smalltalk serve a vital purpose by allowing developers to group related methods within a class, thereby enhancing code readability and maintainability. This organization technique does not affect the runtime behavior of the program but significantly improves the development experience by structuring the class interface in a logical manner.

Categories are purely a development-time aid, utilized within Smalltalk's browsing tools to present a more organized view of a class's methods. It is important to note that categories do not introduce any form of namespace or encapsulation at the code level; they are simply a means of grouping methods visually in development environments.

To define a method within a specific category, Smalltalk developers utilize the development environment's interface. When creating or editing a method, you are prompted to specify a category for the method. Existing categories can be selected, or new categories can be defined on the spot.

Here is an example of how methods might be organized within a class named `Account`:

- **Initialization**: This category could include methods that are responsible for initializing new instances of the `Account` class, such as an initializer that sets up the account balance and account holder's name.

- **Accessing**: Methods that provide access to the object's properties or modify them would fall under this category. For instance, methods to get or set an account's balance would be appropriately stored here.

- **Transaction Handling**: Any methods that deal with transactions, such as depositing or withdrawing money, would be grouped under this category. This categorization helps to keep all transaction-related logic in a centralized location.

When looking up or editing a method in a Smalltalk development environment, the categorization assists in swiftly navigating to the desired method, especially within classes that possess a large number of methods. By adopting a consistent approach to categorization across a project, teams can ensure that their codebases remain navigable and that developers can understand the structure and purpose of classes at a glance.

Although the system of categorizing methods is straightforward, it plays a crucial role in the management of Smalltalk codebases. Effective use of categories can:

- Enhance code readability by logically grouping methods according to their purpose or functionality.
- Facilitate code navigation and maintenance, especially in large and complex classes.
- Promote best practices in coding by encouraging developers to think about the organization and responsibilities of their classes.

While categories do not influence the functionality or performance of Smalltalk applications, they are a powerful tool for code organization. By systematically categorizing methods, developers can create a clearer, more understandable structure within their classes, which pays dividends in terms of code maintainability and developer productivity. Learning to effectively use categories is, therefore, an essential skill for mastering Smalltalk programming.

3.11 Advanced Class Features: Class-side Initialization and Pool Dictionaries

When examining the landscape of Smalltalk's class capabilities, two advanced features stand out for their ability to refine and enhance the execution and organization of code: Class-side Initialization and Pool Dictionaries.

Class-side Initialization is pivotal for setting up class variables before instances of a class are created. This process ensures that class variables are ready with predetermined values that can be utilized across various instances of the class. To initialize class variables, Smalltalk utilizes a special class method typically named `initialize`, which the system automatically calls when the class is first loaded into the system.

Consider the following illustrative example:

```
MyClass class >> initialize
    "Class-side initialization for MyClass"
    Super initialize.
    SomeClassVariable := 'Initial Value'.
```

In the snippet above, the `initialize` method is defined on the class side (indicated by `MyClass class >> initialize`). First, it invokes `Super initialize` to ensure any initialization needed by superclass classes is also performed. Then, it sets a class variable, herein referred to as `SomeClassVariable`, to an initial string value. This pattern is crucial for scenarios where class variables hold resources or configuration that will be used by all instances of the class.

Moving forward, Pool Dictionaries offer a unique mechanism to share constants or global variables across multiple classes without enforcing a superclass-subclass relationship. A Pool Dictionary is essentially a global, named dictionary that any class can declare its usage of, allowing it to access and modify values within the pool. This feature is particularly valuable for managing shared resources or constants in a more modular and controlled manner.

To declare and use a Pool Dictionary, the following steps are undertaken:

- Define a Pool Dictionary. This is typically done in a system browser or a dedicated utility within the Smalltalk development environment.
- Declare the use of the Pool Dictionary in your class or classes. This involves specifying the pool dictionary's name in the class definition.
- Access or modify the values in the Pool Dictionary as needed, using standard dictionary access methods.

Here is how to declare and access a Pool Dictionary named `MyPool`:

```
PoolDictionaries: 'MyPool'.

MyClass >> someMethod
   "Accessing a value from MyPool"
   | someValue |
   someValue := MyPool at: 'SomeKey'.
   ^ someValue
```

In the example above, the class `MyClass` declares it uses `MyPool`, a Pool Dictionary. Inside the method `someMethod`, it then retrieves a value associated with the key `'SomeKey'` from `MyPool`. This illustrative usage showcases how Pool Dictionaries facilitate the shared use of key-value pairs amongst different classes without necessitating direct linkage or inheritance between those classes.

Understanding and employing Class-side Initialization and Pool Dictionaries empowers Smalltalk developers to write cleaner, more modular, and efficient code by properly initializing class variables and sharing constants or configurations among multiple classes in a controlled manner.

3.12 Best Practices for Class and Method Design

In this section, we will discuss the fundamental guidelines and principles that should be adhered to when designing classes and methods in Smalltalk. These best practices are pivotal for creating code that is not only functional but also readable, maintainable, and reusable.

Adhering to the Principle of Least Knowledge

One of the primary recommendations for designing classes and methods involves the Principle of Least Knowledge (also known as Law of Demeter). Essentially, this principle suggests that an object should limit its interactions to a select few closely related objects. This minimizes dependencies and enhances modularity.

For instance, consider you have an object `A` that needs to invoke a method on object `C`, but it gets `C` through an intermediary object `B`. Instead of directly calling a method on `C`, `A` would request `B` to perform the action, which in turn, would call the method on `C`. This avoids creating a direct dependency from `A` to `C`, adhering to the principle and promoting encapsulation.

Naming Conventions

Proper naming conventions are essential for readability and maintainability. Names of classes and methods should be descriptive and reflective of their purpose and functionality. In Smalltalk, it is a common practice to use full descriptive names, even if they are lengthy. For methods, names often include verbs to indicate actions and may follow a pattern that makes the operation's intent clear. For example, a method that checks for the existence of an element might be named `containsElement:`.

```
MyClass>>containsElement: anElement
    ^self elements includes: anElement
```

This method clearly states through its name that it is checking the containment of an element within a collection.

Encapsulation and Data Hiding

Encapsulation is a core component of object-oriented programming. It involves bundling the data (attributes) and methods that operate on the data into single units, or classes, and restricting access to the inner workings of those classes. This is achieved in Smalltalk through the use of instance variables for storing data — these variables should only be accessible through accessor (getter) and mutator (setter) methods if outside access is necessary. For instance:

```
MyClass>>getMyVariable
   ^myVariable

MyClass>>setMyVariable: newValue
  myVariable := newValue
```

These methods provide controlled access to the `myVariable` instance variable, adhering to the encapsulation principle.

Reuse Through Inheritance

Inheritance allows for the creation of a new class (subclass) based on an existing class (superclass), facilitating code reuse and extension. However, it's crucial to use inheritance judiciously. A subclass should embody an "is-a" relationship with its superclass, meaning that it should represent a more specific version of the superclass. Inappropriate use of inheritance can lead to a rigid and fragile system that's hard to maintain. Therefore, favor composition over inheritance unless an "is-a" relationship clearly exists.

Polymorphism and Flexible Design

Polymorphism is an invaluable feature in Smalltalk that enables a method to execute differently based on the object that it is called on. This allows for flexible design where the exact object type does not need to be known by the calling code, enabling the interchangeability of objects as long as they adhere to the expected interface. Make ample use of polymorphism to write code that is decoupled and adaptable to future changes or extensions.

```
Array>>addElement: anElement
   self add: anElement
```

```
LinkedList>>addElement: anElement
   self append: anElement
```

Both `Array` and `LinkedList` may respond to `addElement:` but internally execute different methods (`add:` for an array and `append:` for a linked list).

Documentation and Comments

Documentation and meaningful comments are indispensable components of class and method design. They provide insights into the purpose, usage, expectations, and limitations of your code components. In Smalltalk, comments are placed at the beginning of classes and methods to explain their role and any relevant information that might aid in understanding their functionality. Prioritize clarity and conciseness in your comments to aid future maintainers or users of your code.

Following these best practices will significantly contribute to the development of robust, efficient, and maintainable Smalltalk applications. It's imperative to continually reflect on these guidelines throughout the development process and strive for a balance between adherence to best practices and pragmatic decision-making based on specific project needs.

Chapter 4

Collection Classes in Smalltalk

Handling groups of objects efficiently is essential in any object-oriented programming language, and Smalltalk provides a rich set of collection classes designed for this purpose. This chapter focuses on the diverse range of collection classes available in Smalltalk, including Arrays, Dictionaries, Sets, and Sequences, examining their characteristics, uses, and the operations that can be performed on them. Through understanding these collection classes, readers will gain the ability to manipulate groups of objects with ease, enhancing the sophistication and functionality of their Smalltalk programs.

4.1 Overview of Collection Classes in Smalltalk

Smalltalk's programming paradigm is deeply entrenched in the philosophy of everything being an object. This includes numbers, characters, and even the control structures. Consistent with this philosophy, Smalltalk provides a sophisticated framework for managing collections of objects. A collection in Smalltalk is an object that groups multiple elements, primarily other objects. This section will discuss the fundamental characteristics of collection classes in Smalltalk, providing a foundation for understanding their varied uses and capabilities.

In Smalltalk, collection classes are categorized broadly into several types, each designed to serve distinct purposes and to offer different behaviors and performance characteristics. These classes include:

- **Arrays**: Ordered collections of elements that can be accessed by their index. Arrays are fixed in size upon creation.
- **Dictionaries**: Collections that store elements as key-value pairs. They are ideal for when each stored datum should be retrievable by some unique key.
- **Sets**: Collections of unique elements. They are unordered and do not allow duplicates, making them ideal for ensuring the uniqueness of its elements.
- **Bags**: Similar to sets but allow duplicates. They are unordered collections where elements can occur more than once.
- **OrderedCollections**: Similar to arrays but are dynamic in size. Elements in an ordered collection are indexed and maintain their order.
- **Sequences**: Represent sequential collections that can be accessed sequentially, character strings being a common example.

The choice of collection class depends on the specific needs of the program. For example, if maintaining the order of elements is crucial, an `OrderedCollection` or an `Array` might be most appropriate. If ensuring that each element is unique is vital, a `Set` would be the best choice.

Operations on collections in Smalltalk are powerful and flexible. They allow not just the basic operations such as adding or removing elements but also more complex manipulations like filtering, sorting, and mapping. These operations leverage Smalltalk's block syntax to specify the operation's logic in a concise and expressive manner. For instance, to filter a collection, you could use:

```
collection select: [:element | element isOdd].
```

This line of code would return a new collection containing only the elements from the original collection for which the block returns `true`, in this case selecting only odd elements.

Efficiency and performance considerations are also crucial when working with collection classes. Some operations might be more costly on certain types of collections due to their underlying data structures. For example, accessing an element by index is fast in an `Array` but slow in a `Set`.

In summary, collection classes in Smalltalk are a powerful and essential part of the language's framework for managing groups of objects. By understanding the characteristics, use cases, and operations applicable to each type of collection, you can choose the most appropriate class for your needs and manipulate collections efficiently to enhance your Smalltalk programs. Certainly, moving on with elaborate details for the specified section:

4.2 Using Arrays: Creation, Access, and Manipulation

Arrays in Smalltalk are ordered collections that store objects sequentially. They are one of the simplest and most fundamental collection types, allowing efficient access to elements through index-based retrieval. This section elaborates on the creation, access, and manipulation of arrays in Smalltalk, offering insights into their practical applications.

Creating Arrays

Arrays can be created in several ways in Smalltalk, catering to different needs and contexts. The most direct method is to use the Array class itself. Here are the primary methods:

- Literals: Smalltalk supports array literals using the `#()` syntax. For instance, an array containing integers can be defined as `#(1 2 3 4)`.

- Dynamic creation: To dynamically create arrays, the `Array new: size` method is used, where `size` is the desired number of elements.

- With specific elements: Arrays with predetermined elements can be instantiated using `Array with:` methods. For example, `Array with: 1 with: 2 with: 3` results in an array of three integers.

Accessing Array Elements

Array elements are accessed via their index positions. In Smalltalk, array indices start at 1, contrasting with many programming languages where indices start at 0. The basic syntax for element access is `array at: index`, where `index` is the position of the element. Similarly, to update an element at a specific position, the `array at: index put: newValue` syntax is used. Here's an example demonstrating both access and update:

```
| array |
array := #(1 2 3 4).
"Accessing the second element"
Transcript show: (array at: 2); cr.
"Updating the fourth element"
array at: 4 put: 10.
Transcript show: array.
```

Manipulating Arrays

Arrays in Smalltalk can be manipulated through various operations, including adding, removing, and replacing elements. Some key manipulation methods are:

- Adding elements: Elements can be added to an array using the `add:` method. However, since arrays have a fixed size, it's more common to use a dynamic collection like `OrderedCollection` for collections that need to grow dynamically.
- Copying arrays: The `copy` method creates a shallow copy of the array.
- Concatenating arrays: Arrays can be concatenated using the `,` operator, producing a new array with elements from both arrays.

Example of array manipulation:

```
| array1 array2 concatenatedArray |
array1 := #(1 2 3).
array2 := #(4 5 6).
"Concatenating arrays"
concatenatedArray := array1 , array2.
Transcript show: concatenatedArray.
```

Iterating Over Arrays

Iteration over arrays is performed using loops or collection-specific methods like `do:`. The `do:` method applies a block of code to each element in the array sequentially. Here is an example:

```
| array |
array := #(1 2 3 4 5).
array do: [ :element |
    Transcript show: element printString; cr.
].
```

This section has covered the essentials of using arrays in Smalltalk, including their creation, access, manipulation, and iteration. Mastering these operations is crucial for effective collection management in

Smalltalk, as arrays are often the backbone of data structure strategies in applications.

4.3 Understanding Ordered and Unordered Collections

In Smalltalk, a fundamental categorization among collection classes is between ordered and unordered collections. This distinction plays a critical role in how collections are used and managed within the programming environment.

Ordered Collections

An ordered collection, as the name suggests, maintains the order in which elements are added. This feature is crucial when the sequence of elements impacts the outcome of operations performed on the collection.

The `OrderedCollection` class is the standard representation of ordered collections in Smalltalk. Elements in an `OrderedCollection` can be accessed, added, or removed based on their position within the collection. The first element is at position 1, the second at position 2, and so forth, adhering to Smalltalk's 1-based indexing.

To illustrate the creation and manipulation of an `OrderedCollection`, consider the following example:

```
| orderedCollection |
orderedCollection := OrderedCollection new.
orderedCollection add: 'Apple'; add: 'Banana'; add: 'Cherry'.
```

In the above example, an `OrderedCollection` instance is created and populated with three elements. The order in which these elements are added is preserved by the collection.

Accessing an element by its position can be done as follows:

```
| fruit |
```

```
fruit := orderedCollection at: 2.
```

This snippet fetches the second element in the collection, which would yield 'Banana'.

The ability to insert elements at a specific position is another feature of ordered collections. The following example demonstrates inserting an element at the second position:

```
orderedCollection add: 'Blueberry' at: 2.
```

After executing the above, the collection's order will be: 'Apple', 'Blueberry', 'Banana', 'Cherry'.

Unordered Collections

Unordered collections, on the other hand, do not maintain any specific order among their elements. The `Set` and `Bag` classes are typical examples of unordered collections in Smalltalk. These collections are optimized for fast access and manipulation of elements without regard to the sequence in which they were added.

The `Set` class ensures that each element is unique within the collection. In contrast, a `Bag` allows duplicate elements but, like a `Set`, does not preserve the order of elements.

Below is an example demonstrating the creation of a `Set`:

```
| aSet |
aSet := Set new.
aSet add: 'Apple'; add: 'Banana'; add: 'Apple'.
```

In this case, attempting to add 'Apple' a second time to the `Set` has no effect, as a `Set` does not allow duplicates. The final composition of a`Set` would be 'Apple', 'Banana'.

Choosing Between Ordered and Unordered Collections

The choice between using an ordered or unordered collection hinges on the specific requirements of the application. If maintaining the sequence of elements is essential, an OrderedCollection would be the appropriate choice. Conversely, when the uniqueness of elements is a priority, and order is irrelevant, a Set would be more suitable. Understanding these distinctions and the characteristics of each collection type enables developers to employ the most effective data structures for their respective needs, thus enhancing the efficiency and readability of their Smalltalk programs.

4.4 Working with Dictionaries for Key-Value Pair Storage

Dictionaries in Smalltalk serve a crucial role in storing elements as key-value pairs. This structure facilitates the retrieval of values based on unique keys, enabling efficient data lookup and manipulation. A key feature distinguishing dictionaries from other collection classes is their ability to manage associations (key-value pairs) rather than mere values. This section elucidates the creation, manipulation, and practical applications of dictionaries in Smalltalk.

Creating a dictionary is straightforward. The Smalltalk language provides a class named Dictionary, which is utilized to instantiate a new dictionary object. The following example demonstrates this:

```
| myDictionary |
myDictionary := Dictionary new.
```

Upon creation, a dictionary is empty. To populate it, keys are associated with respective values using the message at:put:. Here is how one can add a key-value pair to myDictionary:

```
myDictionary at: #key1 put: 'Smalltalk'.
```

In the example above, #key1 represents a symbol serving as the key, and the string 'Smalltalk' is the value associated with this key. Symbols are commonly used as keys in dictionaries due to their uniqueness and immutability.

Retrieving a value from a dictionary requires the use of the key associated with the value of interest. The at: message is employed for this purpose:

```
| valueForKey1 |
valueForKey1 := myDictionary at: #key1.
```

The above snippet searches for the key `#key1` within `myDictionary` and assigns the corresponding value ('Smalltalk') to `valueForKey1`.

Dictionaries also provide methods to remove key-value pairs. The `removeKey:` message, for example, removes the pair associated with the specified key:

```
myDictionary removeKey: #key1.
```

After execution of the above code, `myDictionary` would no longer contain the key-value pair associated with `#key1`.

To iterate over all key-value pairs in a dictionary, Smalltalk provides various enumeration messages. The following example demonstrates the use of `do:` to iterate over each association in a dictionary:

```
myDictionary at: #key1 put: 'Value 1'.
myDictionary at: #key2 put: 'Value 2'.
myDictionary do: [:each | Transcript show: each key, ' maps to ', each value; cr
    ].
```

In this snippet, `myDictionary` is populated with two key-value pairs. The `do:` message sends a block (anonymous function) that takes each association in the dictionary. The block prints each key-value pair to the Transcript, illustrating the mapping between keys and values.

Efficiently handling exceptions related to key absence is vital when working with dictionaries. Attempting to access a value for a nonexistent key using `at:` will result in an error. To safely handle such cases, `at:ifAbsent:` can be used:

```
| valueForMissingKey |
valueForMissingKey := myDictionary at: #missingKey ifAbsent: ['Key not found'].
```

In the example above, if `#missingKey` is not present in `myDictionary`, the string 'Key not found' is returned instead of raising an error.

Dictionaries in Smalltalk are a powerful mechanism for managing data as key-value pairs, offering efficient data storage, retrieval, and manipulation capabilities. Mastery of dictionaries enhances a developer's ability to handle complex data structures and contributes significantly to writing sophisticated Smalltalk programs.

4.5 Sets and Bags: Usage and Differences

Sets and Bags in Smalltalk serve as collection classes that manage groups of objects. While they share similarities, such as both being unordered collections, their unique characteristics and use cases distinguish them significantly.

Understanding Sets

A `Set` in Smalltalk is a collection that holds a unique set of elements. This means no two elements in a `Set` are identical. `Sets` are particularly useful when the uniqueness of elements is paramount, and the order of elements is irrelevant.

```
| setExample |
setExample := Set new.
setExample add: 'Smalltalk'.
setExample add: 'Programming'.
setExample add: 'Smalltalk'. "Adding 'Smalltalk' again has no effect"
```

In the code snippet above, attempting to add the string 'Smalltalk' a second time to the `Set` named `setExample` has no effect because a `Set` automatically ensures that only unique elements are stored.

Understanding Bags

A `Bag`, on the other hand, is similar to a `Set` but allows duplicate elements. Thus, if your application logic requires the collection of objects where duplicates are meaningful, a `Bag` would be the appropriate choice.

```
| bagExample |
bagExample := Bag new.
bagExample add: 'Smalltalk'.
bagExample add: 'Programming'.
bagExample add: 'Smalltalk'. "This time 'Smalltalk' is added again"
```

In this case, adding 'Smalltalk' twice to the Bag named `bagExample` is perfectly valid, and the Bag will contain two instances of 'Smalltalk'.

Using Sets and Bags

The choice between using a `Set` and a `Bag` depends on the specific requirements of your application. Below are bullets highlighting their typical uses:

- Use `Sets` when you need to ensure all elements are unique.
- Use `Bags` when duplicates are meaningful and should be counted.

For example, if you are counting the occurrences of words in a document, a `Bag` would allow easy accumulation of counts for each word, whereas a `Set` could be used to simply determine which words appear in the document, regardless of frequency.

Sorting and Iterating

Neither `Sets` nor `Bags` maintain their elements in a specific order. However, it is possible to convert them to ordered collections if sorting or specific iteration order is required.

```
| sortedSetExample bagExample sortedBagExample |
setExample := Set withAll: {'Smalltalk'. 'Programming'. 'Guide'}.
sortedSetExample := setExample asSortedCollection.

bagExample := Bag withAll: {'Smalltalk'. 'Programming'. 'Smalltalk'}.
sortedBagExample := bagExample asSortedCollection.
```

By sending the message `asSortedCollection` to either a `Set` or a `Bag`, you can obtain a new collection where elements are sorted, facilitating ordered iteration.

In summary, understanding the difference between `Sets` and `Bags` and their appropriate uses enhances the flexibility and efficiency of managing groupings of objects in Smalltalk. Whether enforcing uniqueness or accounting for duplicates, these collection classes offer robust options for sophisticated data handling

4.6 Sequences, Strings, and Character Collections

Sequences in Smalltalk serve as ordered collections in which elements are indexed numerically, starting from one. This allows for precise control over the position of each element. Commonly used sequence types include `Array`, `OrderedCollection`, and `String`. Each of these collections maintains its elements in a specific sequence, which is a cornerstone for many programming tasks, ranging from text processing to complex data manipulation.

Strings and Character collections are particularly important types of sequences because they deal with textual data. A `String` in Smalltalk is essentially an array of characters, enabling operations such as concatenation, substring extraction, and pattern matching.

Manipulating Strings and Characters

Given the importance of strings in programming, Smalltalk offers a robust set of operations for string manipulation. These operations can be categorized into creation, access, and modification.

- **Creation:** New strings can be created directly by enclosing the text in single quotes. For instance, `'Hello, World!'` is a string containing the traditional greeting.

- **Access:** Individual characters within a string can be accessed using the `at:` message. For example, `'Smalltalk'at: 1` returns the character `S`.

- **Modification:** Strings in Smalltalk are immutable; however, modifications can be achieved by creating a new string. For instance, concatenation is performed using the `,` operator: `'Small', 'talk'` results in `'Smalltalk'`.

Character Collections

Collections of characters, such as `CharacterSet`, offer specialized utilities for dealing with groups of characters. For instance, defining a collection of vowels can be achieved as follows:

```
CharacterSet vowels := CharacterSet with: $a with: $e with: $i with: $o with: $u.
```

This `CharacterSet` can then be used to perform operations such as checking if a character is a vowel, which is significantly more efficient than manual comparison.

Working with Sequences

Sequences, including strings, can be manipulated using a variety of built-in methods. To iterate over each character in a string and perform an operation, Smalltalk provides the `do:` method. Here is an example that counts the number of vowels in a string:

```
String vowelsInString: aString
    | vowels count |
    vowels := CharacterSet vowels.
    count := 0.
    aString do: [:char | (vowels includes: char) ifTrue: [count := count + 1]].
    ^count
```

This method demonstrates several key features of working with sequences in Smalltalk, including collection iteration and conditional logic within blocks.

Advanced String Operations

Beyond basic manipulation, Smalltalk strings support a variety of advanced operations, facilitating tasks such as pattern matching and replacement. For example, to find and replace all occurrences of a substring within a string, one can use the `subStrings:` method combined with replacement logic. However, due to the immutable nature of strings, remember that each manipulation results in the creation of a new string.

```
'Smalltalk programming'.subStrings: 'programming' with: 'coding'
```

This operation would yield the new string `'Smalltalk coding'`, demonstrating the ease with which text manipulation can be achieved in Smalltalk.

Combining these string and character manipulation techniques enables the development of complex and powerful text-processing features in Smalltalk applications, from simple data entry forms to sophisticated natural language processing systems.

4.7 Using Streams for Sequential Access

In this section we will discuss the use of streams in Smalltalk for the sequential access of collection elements. Streams provide a way to iterate over collections, both for reading and writing, in a sequential manner. This is particularly useful for managing collections where the order of elements matters or when working with large data sets where random access is not efficient or possible.

Streams in Smalltalk are divided into two main types: ReadStream and WriteStream. As their names suggest, ReadStream is used for reading data from collections, while WriteStream is used for writing data to collections. There is also a third type, named ReadWriteStream, which combines the functionalities of both ReadStream and WriteStream, allowing for both reading from and writing to collections.

Creating and Using ReadStreams

To create a ReadStream on a collection, one typically sends the message `readStream` to that collection. The following example demonstrates creating a ReadStream on an Array.

```
| array stream |
array := #('Smalltalk' 'is' 'powerful').
stream := array readStream.
```

Once a ReadStream is created, elements can be accessed sequentially using the `next` message, which returns the next element in the stream and advances the stream's position. Here's an example:

```
| nextElement |
nextElement := stream next. "This will return 'Smalltalk'"
```

The `atEnd` message can be used to check if the stream has reached the end of the collection, as illustrated below:

```
| allElements |
allElements := OrderedCollection new.
[stream atEnd] whileFalse: [allElements add: stream next].
```

This code snippet will sequentially read all elements from the stream and collect them in an OrderedCollection.

Utilizing WriteStreams

A WriteStream is created similarly to a ReadStream but by sending the message `writeStream` to a collection. Here's how to create and use a WriteStream on an Array.

```
| array stream |
array := Array new: 10.
stream := array writeStream.
```

To write data into the collection, use the `nextPut:` message. For example, to write the string 'Hello' into the stream:

```
stream nextPut: 'Hello'.
```

For writing multiple elements at once, the `nextPutAll:` message can be used:

```
stream nextPutAll: #('Smalltalk' 'Programming').
```

Combining Read and Write Operations with ReadWriteStream

ReadWriteStream allows for both reading from and writing to a collection. It is particularly useful for cases where a collection needs to be modified while it is being read. The creation and basic operations are analogous to those of ReadStream and WriteStream but combine their functionalities.

Closing Remarks

Streams offer a powerful means for sequential data access and manipulation in Smalltalk. Understanding how to use ReadStream, WriteStream, and ReadWriteStream is critical for efficient collection management, especially in scenarios requiring sequential processing of data. Remember that while streams are extremely useful for sequential access, selecting the appropriate collection class and access method based on the specific needs of your application is equally essential for optimizing performance and resource utilization.

4.8 Collection Iteration: Enumeration and Iterators

Collection iteration in Smalltalk is primarily facilitated through enumeration and iterators, which are powerful tools that enable developers to traverse, access, and manipulate elements within collection classes effectively. This section will discuss the mechanisms and techniques used for iterating over different types of collections such as Arrays, Dictionaries, Sets, and Sequences, providing insights into their effective usage for performing a range of operations.

Enumerating collections in Smalltalk can be accomplished using various messages that collections understand, such as `do:`, `collect:`, `select:`, `reject:`, `inject:into:`, among others. These messages allow iteration over the elements of a collection without requiring explicit management of the iteration's state, such as indexes or keys, thus simplifying code and enhancing readability.

```
"Example of using the do: message to iterate over an Array"
#(1 2 3 4 5) do: [:element | Transcript show: element printString, ' '].
```

```
Output:
1 2 3 4 5
```

This example demonstrates using the `do:` message with an anonymous function (block) that takes each element of the Array and prints it. The `Transcript` is a Smalltalk global object used for output.

Iterators offer a different approach to collection iteration. While enumeration with messages abstracts the iteration process entirely, iterators provide a means to explicitly control the iteration flow. Smalltalk's iterator protocol includes messages such as `next`, `atEnd`, and `reset`. An iterator is obtained from a collection and then used to traverse the collection one element at a time.

```
"Example of using an Iterator to iterate over an Array"
| array iterator |
array := #(1 2 3 4 5).
iterator := array iterator.
[iterator atEnd] whileFalse: [
    Transcript show: (iterator next) printString, ' '].
```

```
Output:
1 2 3 4 5
```

In this example, `iterator` is an object obtained from the Array array that allows for explicit iteration over its elements. The message `atEnd` checks if the iterator has reached the end of the collection, while `next` moves the iterator to the next element and returns it. Using iterators gives more control over the iteration process, enabling operations such as pausing, resuming, or even reversing the iteration sequence, albeit with a slightly more complex syntax.

- The `do:` message and similar enumeration messages provide a concise, high-level interface for iterating collections without the need to manage iteration state explicitly.
- Iterators offer more granular control over the iteration process and can be particularly useful in scenarios requiring complex iteration logic.

When selecting between enumeration and iterators for collection iteration in Smalltalk, the choice depends on the specific requirements of the task at hand. Enumeration messages offer simplicity and elegance, suitable for most common iteration scenarios. In contrast, iterators provide additional control and flexibility, which may be necessary for more complex or non-linear iteration patterns. Understanding both approaches allows Smalltalk developers to leverage the full potential of collection classes in building sophisticated and efficient object-oriented applications.

4.9 Sorting Collections: Techniques and Custom Sorts

Sorting is a fundamental operation when working with collections in Smalltalk, enabling the organization of objects in a predefined order. This section will discuss the mechanisms available in Smalltalk for sorting collections, ranging from built-in sorting methods to implementing custom sorting logic using blocks.

Smalltalk's collection classes come with built-in sorting methods that are sufficient for many common scenarios. For instance, the `sort` method, available in most collection classes, automatically sorts the collection in ascending order based on the natural ordering of its elements. The implementation of this method is straightforward, as demonstrated in the following example where we sort an array of integers.

```
| numbers sortedNumbers |
numbers := #(3 1 4 1 5 9 2 6). % Necessary LaTeX escaping: Hash symbol (#) in
    this context is a literal character and does not start a comment.
sortedNumbers := numbers sort.
```

To observe the result of this operation, inspecting `sortedNumbers` produces the sorted array.

```
#(1 1 2 3 4 5 6 9)
```

While the `sort` method works well for collections of objects with a clear natural ordering (such as integers or strings), the need often arises to sort collections based on custom criteria. For this purpose, Smalltalk provides the `sorted:` method, which takes a block as its argument. This block specifies the sorting logic, accepting two elements from the collection and returning true if the first element should come before the second in the sorted collection.

For example, consider a collection of strings that we wish to sort based on their lengths rather than lexicographically. The following code demonstrates the use of the `sorted:` method for this purpose.

```
| strings sortedByLength |
strings := #('Smalltalk' 'is' 'awesome' '!' 'Programming' 'in').
sortedByLength := strings sorted: [:a :b | a size < b size].
```

Inspecting `sortedByLength` yields the strings sorted by their lengths.

```
#('!' 'is' 'in' 'awesome' 'Smalltalk' 'Programming')
```

This approach grants significant flexibility, allowing for sorting based on complex criteria or custom comparison methods between objects.

To sort collections in descending order or according to multiple criteria, the sorting block can be adjusted accordingly. For instance, to sort a collection of dictionaries representing students by their scores in descending order, and then by name in ascending order when scores are equal, the sorting logic would compare the scores and, if necessary, the names.

When implementing custom sorts, understanding the performance implications is critical. Smalltalk's sorting algorithms are designed to be efficient, but the computational cost of the block used for comparison can impact overall performance, especially for large collections. It's advisable to keep the comparison logic as simple as possible and consider pre-processing the collection if the sorting criteria are computationally intensive.

Smalltalk's collection classes offer robust mechanisms for sorting, from simple natural order sorting to complex custom sorts implemented with blocks. By leveraging these tools, you can effectively manipulate and organize collections, thereby enhancing the functionality and efficiency of your Smalltalk programs.

4.10 Using Blocks with Collections for Filtering and Mapping

Blocks in Smalltalk serve a significant role in enabling functional programming patterns, particularly in the context of collections. Using blocks, developers can succinctly encode complex operations like filtering and mapping over collections. This section delves into the specifics of employing blocks with Smalltalk's collection classes to accomplish these tasks.

Filtering Collections with Blocks

Filtering involves iterating over a collection and selecting elements that satisfy a given condition. In Smalltalk, this is accomplished using the `select:` method, which accepts a block as an argument. The block defines the condition and is applied to each element of the collection. Only the elements for which the block evaluates to `true` are included in the resulting collection.

Consider the following example where we have an array of numbers and we want to filter out only the even numbers:

```
| numbers evenNumbers |
```

```
numbers := #(2 5 8 1 10).
evenNumbers := numbers select: [:each | each even].
```

In this example, the `select:` method is sent to the array `numbers` with a block. The block `[:each | each even]` is executed for each element in the array. The `even` message sent to each number returns `true` for even numbers, thus, `evenNumbers` would contain `#(2 8 10)` after the operation.

Mapping Collections with Blocks

Mapping transforms each element in a collection according to a specified rule or function. The `collect:` method is used for this purpose in Smalltalk, taking a block that describes how each element should be transformed. The output is a new collection of transformed elements.

For illustration, assume we wish to square each number in an array:

```
| numbers squaredNumbers |
numbers := #(1 2 3 4).
squaredNumbers := numbers collect: [:each | each squared].
```

Here, `collect:` traverses the `numbers` array, applying the block `[:each | each squared]` to each number. This block calculates the square of each number, producing `#(1 4 9 16)` stored in `squaredNumbers`.

Both filtering and mapping are powerful tools for working with collections in Smalltalk. They allow for the concise expression of complex operations without the need for explicit loops or temporary variables. Furthermore, these operations can be combined as needed. For instance, to filter a collection and then map the results, one could chain the `select:` and `collect:` methods together:

```
| numbers evenNumbersSquared |
numbers := #(2 5 8 1 10).
evenNumbersSquared := numbers select: [:each | each even] collect: [:each | each
    squared].
```

This code filters `numbers` to retain only even ones and then maps over the filtered collection to square each number. The final result, stored in `evenNumbersSquared`, would be `#(4 64 100)`, demonstrating the elegance and power of combining filtering and mapping operations in Smalltalk.

Best Practices for Using Blocks with Collections

While using blocks with collections is highly expressive and efficient, there are best practices to ensure code maintainability and performance:

- Use meaningful names for block parameters to enhance code readability.
- When chaining multiple operations, consider the impact on performance and memory usage, particularly for large collections.
- Utilize Smalltalk's rich collection of block-based methods, such as `reject:`, `inject:into:`, and `detect:ifNone:`, to further leverage the language's expressive power.

In summary, blocks empower Smalltalk developers to write concise yet powerful collection manipulation code via filtering and mapping. Mastering the use of blocks with collections is a pivotal skill for any Smalltalk programmer, facilitating the creation of expressive, functional-style code that is both readable and efficient.

4.11 Best Practices for Collection Management

Effective management of collections in Smalltalk not only ensures optimal performance of applications but also enhances code readability and maintainability. This section delineates several best practices for managing collection classes, drawing from established conventions and the rich functionality Smalltalk provides.

- **Select the Appropriate Collection Type**: The first step in efficient collection management is choosing the right type of collection. Smalltalk offers a variety of collection classes, each designed for specific use cases. For example, use `Array` for ordered collections of fixed size, `OrderedCollection` for ordered collections of variable size, `Dictionary` for key-value pairs, and `Set` for unique elements. Making an informed decision about which collection type to use based on the needs of your program can significantly impact its performance and scalability.

- **Leverage Lazy Evaluation with Streams**: When working with large collections or files, consider using `Stream` objects to process data lazily. This means data will only be processed as needed, rather than all at once, which can lead to substantial performance improvements and lower memory consumption. Here's an example of using streams:

```
| largeCollection streamResult |
largeCollection := 1 to: 1000000.
streamResult := largeCollection readStream collect: [:each | each * 2].
```

  In the example above, `readStream` creates a stream over `largeCollection`, and `collect:` processes elements lazily.

- **Use Blocks Efficiently for Collection Operations**: Smalltalk's collections provide powerful methods that take blocks (anonymous functions) as arguments, enabling concise and expressive manipulation of collections. However, it is essential to use them judiciously to avoid unnecessary performance overhead. For example, prefer direct collection manipulation methods over generic iterations when possible:

```
"Less efficient"
collection do: [:each | each performOperation].
"More efficient"
collection performOperation.
```

- **Utilize Copying for Mutable Collections**: When working with mutable collections that may change over time, consider copying the collection before performing operations that do not intend to alter the original collection. This practice helps prevent unintended side effects. For instance:

```
| originalCollection copiedCollection |
originalCollection := OrderedCollection withAll: {1. 2. 3}.
copiedCollection := originalCollection copy.
copiedCollection add: 4. "originalCollection remains unchanged"
```

- **Opt for Bulk Operations When Possible**: Many collection classes in Smalltalk support bulk operations, such as `addAll:`, `removeAll:`, etc. Utilizing these methods can dramatically enhance performance over iterating through elements and adding or removing them one by one, especially for large collections.

- **Employ Iteration Protocols Wisely**: Smalltalk provides a rich set of iteration protocols. While `do:` is the most basic iteration method, others like `select:`, `collect:`, `reject:`, and `inject:into:` can often accomplish the same tasks more expressively and with less code. Selecting the appropriate iteration method can significantly simplify code.

```
| collection evenNumbers |
collection := 1 to: 10.
evenNumbers := collection select: [:each | each even].
```

- **Regularly Purge Unused Collections**: In dynamic and long-running Smalltalk applications, it's crucial to regularly review and dispose of unused collections to free up memory. Employing `WeakArray` or `WeakSet` for temporary collections can help as they allow their elements to be garbage collected when no longer in use.

- **Analyze Collection Performance**: Lastly, always measure the performance implications of your collection management tactics. Smalltalk environments typically provide tools for profiling and debugging, which can be used to identify and optimize bottlenecks related to collection usage.

In summary, managing collections effectively is a multifaceted process that requires careful consideration of the type of collection, the operations performed, and the overall impact on application performance and memory usage. By adhering to the best practices outlined above, developers can ensure that their use of Smalltalk's rich collection classes is both efficient and maintainable.

4.12 Common Pitfalls with Collections and How to Avoid Them

While working with collection classes in Smalltalk, several common pitfalls may hinder the efficiency and correctness of your programs. Recognizing and understanding how to avoid these pitfalls is crucial for developing robust and efficient Smalltalk code.

Modifying Collections During Iteration

One frequent mistake is modifying a collection (e.g., adding or removing elements) while iterating over it. This can lead to unpredictable behavior or runtime errors. To avoid this pitfall, it is advisable to collect the items to be modified in a separate collection first, then apply the modifications after the iteration.

```
"Example of modifying a collection safely"
| toRemove collection |
collection := OrderedCollection withAll: #(1 2 3 4 5).
toRemove := collection select: [:each | each isEven].

toRemove do: [:each | collection remove: each].
```

Ignoring Collection Capacity

Not managing the capacity of dynamic collections correctly can lead to performance issues. For large collections, it is more efficient to initialize the collection with a capacity close to its expected size.

```
"Efficiently initializing a large collection"
| largeCollection |
largeCollection := OrderedCollection new: 10000.
```

Choosing the Wrong Collection Type

Selecting an inappropriate collection type for the task can significantly impact performance and functionality. For instance, using an Array when frequent insertion and deletion operations are expected is less efficient than using a LinkedList. Understanding the characteristics of each collection type is vital for their effective use.

- Use `Array` for fixed-size collections.
- Use `OrderedCollection` or `LinkedList` for collections requiring frequent insertions and deletions.
- Use `Dictionary` for key-value pair storage.
- Use `Set` for unique element storage without concern for order.

Failing to Utilize Convenience Methods

Smalltalk collections offer a wide range of convenience methods for common operations, such as filtering, mapping, and reducing. Neglecting these methods in favor of manual implementations can lead to more verbose and less efficient code.

```
"Using convenience methods for filtering"
| collection evenNumbers |
collection := #(1 2 3 4 5 6 7 8).
evenNumbers := collection select: [:each | each isEven].
```

Overlooking Collection Immutability

Some collection instances, particularly those returned by certain methods, may be immutable. Attempting to modify such collections will result in runtime errors. Always verify whether a collection is mutable before attempting to change it.

Improper Use of Comparisons and Hashing

When working with collections such as Sets or Dictionaries, which rely on hashing and equality comparisons, ensure that the objects stored in these collections properly implement `hash` and `=` (`equals`) methods. Failure to do so can lead to incorrect behavior during collection operations.

To conclude, while Smalltalk's collection classes provide powerful tools for managing groups of objects, being aware of and avoiding the common pitfalls discussed is essential for writing efficient and bug-free code. Implementing the recommended practices will lead to more reliable, maintainable, and performant Smalltalk applications.

Chapter 5

Smalltalk Block Closures and Control Structures

Smalltalk's block closures and control structures offer powerful mechanisms for controlling flow and encapsulating units of work as objects. This chapter delves into how block closures function as first-class citizens in Smalltalk, allowing for sophisticated control structures, including conditionals, loops, and iterations over collections. Readers will learn to leverage these constructs to write concise, expressive code that effectively manages program execution flow, embodying the principles of compactness and reusability that are central to effective Smalltalk programming.

5.1 Introduction to Blocks and Closures

Blocks in Smalltalk embody a powerful construct, serving as the cornerstone for encapsulating and deferring execution of code snippets. Unlike many programming languages where functions or methods are the primary means of code unit encapsulation, Smalltalk leverages blocks as an integral part of its language design, offering a more granular and flexible approach to code execution management.

A block in Smalltalk is essentially an anonymous function that can be passed around as a first-class citizen; that is, it can be assigned to variables, passed as arguments to functions (or, in Smalltalk parlance, messages), and returned from messages. Blocks are enclosed in square brackets, '[ ]', and can contain local variable declarations, control structures, and any valid Smalltalk expressions.

To instantiate a block, simply encapsulate the desired code within square brackets. For example:

```
[Transcript show: 'Hello, Smalltalk!']
```

This block, when executed, will display the string "Hello, Smalltalk!" in the Transcript (a Smalltalk tool for output).

Blocks can be executed by sending them the message 'value', 'value:', 'value:value:', etc., depending on the number of arguments they expect. A block without parameters is executed with the 'value' message as shown below:

```
|[Transcript show: 'Executing a block']. value|
```

The output of the above block execution will be:

```
Executing a block
```

Another distinguishing feature of blocks is their support for closure. A closure is a block that captures and retains the surrounding lexical context in which it is defined. This means that a block can access and manipulate variables from its enclosing scope, even after that scope has exited. This property allows for a higher degree of functionality and flexibility in managing the flow of execution and storing state in a concise manner.

For instance, consider a block that increments a counter:

```
|counter incrementBlock|
counter := 0.
incrementBlock := [counter := counter + 1].
incrementBlock value.
incrementBlock value.
Transcript show: 'Counter: ', counter printString.
```

This will output:

```
Counter: 2
```

Through this mechanism, blocks in Smalltalk provide a powerful tool for not only deferring execution but also for enclosing state and behavior in a portable, encapsulated unit of code. This capability forms the bedrock of more advanced control structures and patterns in Smalltalk, which we will explore in the following sections.

5.2 Defining and Using Blocks

Blocks in Smalltalk are anonymous functions or closures, which are essential for various control structures and iteration patterns. A block is essentially a chunk of code that can be executed at a later time. This section will explain the syntax for defining blocks, how they can be invoked, and their practical usage.

Syntax for Defining Blocks

A block is defined by enclosing the code within square brackets. The syntax is straightforward:

```
[blockVariable := [code to execute]].
```

Here is an example of a simple block that prints a message:

```
helloBlock := [Transcript show: 'Hello, Smalltalk!'].
```

Invoking Blocks

To execute the code within a block, you send the block the `value` message. Consider the `helloBlock` defined earlier; it can be invoked as follows:

```
helloBlock value.
```

This will result in the output:

```
Hello, Smalltalk!
```

Passing Parameters to Blocks

Blocks can also accept parameters. The syntax for defining a block with parameters involves adding a colon (:) followed by a parameter name between the vertical bars (| |) at the beginning of the block. After the vertical bars, you provide the block's code which can utilize these parameters. Here is how to define and use such a block:

```
greetBlock := [:name | Transcript show: 'Hello, ', name, '!'].
```

To invoke this block with a parameter:

```
greetBlock value: 'Alice'.
```

This will produce:

```
Hello, Alice!
```

Blocks with Multiple Parameters

Blocks can accept multiple parameters. To define a block with multiple parameters, separate each parameter name with a colon. For example:

```
additionBlock := [:a :b | a + b].
```

This block takes two parameters and returns their sum. It can be invoked as follows:

```
sum := additionBlock value: 5 value: 7.
Transcript show: sum printString.
```

This will print:

```
12
```

Using Blocks for Code Organization

Blocks can effectively organize and manage code in Smalltalk. They enable creating modular code chunks that can be reused and executed based on the program's logic. For example, a block could encapsulate a complex computation or a sequence of operations that are repeated in various parts of an application.

Practical Usage of Blocks

Practically, blocks are used in Smalltalk for iterating over collections, handling exceptions, and implementing conditional statements and loops. Their ability to capture and carry the surrounding context makes them powerful tools for writing expressive and compact code.

Understanding how to define and use blocks in Smalltalk is fundamental to mastering the language. Blocks not only offer a way to encapsulate functionality but also serve as the basis for control structures and iteration over collections, showcasing the elegance and simplicity of Smalltalk programming.

5.3 Variables Scope within Blocks

Understanding the scope of variables within blocks is crucial for mastering Smalltalk programming. In Smalltalk, blocks are not just simple control structures; they are first-class objects that can be passed around, stored in variables, and executed dynamically. This flexibility comes with its nuances, particularly concerning variable scope. In this section, we will dissect how variable scopes are delineated within blocks and the implications for programming practices.

A variable's scope determines where within a program that variable can be accessed. Smalltalk delineates between global, class, instance, and local variables, each with its accessibility rules. However, when it comes to blocks, the scoping rules take on an additional layer of complexity.

There are three primary types of variables to consider in the context of blocks:

- Local variables: Declared within a block and accessible only inside that block.
- Outer variables: Variables that are not local but are accessible within the block because they are part of an enclosing method or block.
- Global and class variables: Accessible from anywhere in the program, including within blocks.

To illustrate how these scopes interact, let's consider an example:

```
| outerVariable |
outerVariable := 10.
[ | blockVariable |
  blockVariable := 5.
  Transcript show: (outerVariable + blockVariable) printString.
] value.
```

In this example, 'outerVariable' is an outer variable relative to the block, whereas 'blockVariable' is local to the block it is defined in. The block is able to access 'outerVariable' because it is defined in the enclosing method's scope. This access is possible due to the lexical scope rules of Smalltalk, which allow blocks to capture and retain references to outer variables present in their lexical environment at the time of their definition.

The interaction between blocks and variable scope can also lead to closures, a powerful but more complex topic covered in a later section. For now, it is sufficient to understand that when a block captures outer variables, it retains not just their values but references to the variables themselves. This means changes to those variables by the block will be reflected in the enclosing scope.

Consider an example demonstrating this:

```
| outerVariable block |
```

```
outerVariable := 10.
block := [ outerVariable := 20 ].
block value.
Transcript show: outerVariable printString. "This will print 20"
```

When the block is executed, it modifies 'outerVariable' from the outer scope. This change is reflected when 'outerVariable' is accessed afterward, underscoring the dynamic scoping mechanism at play.

It is essential to manage variable scope within blocks carefully to avoid unintended side effects. Specifically, the inadvertent modification of outer variables from within a block can lead to bugs that are difficult to trace. Therefore, understanding and controlling variable scope is a critical skill in Smalltalk programming.

To conclude, the scope of variables within Smalltalk blocks is a nuanced aspect that combines lexical scoping with the dynamic capabilities of blocks. By grasiting these concepts, programmers can utilize blocks more effectively, harnessing their full potential for creating concise, flexible, and powerful Smalltalk code.

5.4 Blocks as Arguments: Higher-Order Messaging

Blocks in Smalltalk hold a unique position, not just as chunks of code to be executed, but as objects that can be passed around, stored, and manipulated. This capability is particularly powerful when blocks are used as arguments in method calls, enabling what is known as higher-order messaging.

Higher-order messaging refers to the ability to treat functions—or in the context of Smalltalk, blocks—as values that can be passed to other functions or methods. This allows for a high degree of abstraction and reusability, as the same piece of code can operate on different blocks, which encapsulate different actions or computations.

Basic Syntax of Passing Blocks as Arguments

The syntax for passing a block as an argument is straightforward. Consider the do: method, which is a common way to iterate over collections in Smalltalk. This method accepts a block as its argument and executes the block once for each element in the collection.

```
aCollection do: [:each | Transcript show: each printString; cr].
```

In this example, the block `[:each | Transcript show: each printString; cr]` is passed to the `do:` method of `aCollection`. For each element in `aCollection`, the block is executed with `each` bound to the current element.

Higher-Order Methods and Blocks

Smalltalk's standard library provides several methods that take blocks as arguments, facilitating powerful operations such as filtering, mapping, and reducing collections without the need for explicit loops. These methods abstract away the mechanics of iteration, focusing instead on what should be done with each element.

- `collect:` — Transforms each element of a collection using the block and returns a new collection of the results.
- `select:` — Returns a new collection containing all elements for which the block evaluates to true.
- `reject:` — The opposite of `select:`, this method returns a new collection of elements for which the block evaluates to false.
- `detect:` — Finds the first element in a collection for which the block evaluates to true.

Example: Using Blocks for Filtering

To illustrate the power of passing blocks as arguments, consider the following example where we filter a collection of numbers to find only the even ones:

```
numbers := #(1 2 3 4 5 6 7 8 9 10).
evenNumbers := numbers select: [:each | (each \\ 2) = 0].
```

In this case, `select:` is passed a block that returns `true` for even numbers. The result, `evenNumbers`, is a collection `#(2 4 6 8 10)`.

Advantages of Higher-Order Messaging

Using blocks as arguments for higher-order messaging provides several benefits:

- **Abstraction and Reusability:** By encapsulating actions in blocks, you can write more abstract and reusable code, reducing duplication and improving maintainability.
- **Expressiveness:** Higher-order messaging allows for more expressive code that closely models the problem domain, making it easier to understand and modify.
- **Flexibility:** Since blocks can capture and abstract any action or computation, you have the flexibility to pass complex operations as arguments with minimal syntax.

The use of blocks as arguments for higher-order messaging in Smalltalk is a powerful feature that promotes abstraction, reusability, and expressiveness in code. By leveraging this feature, Smalltalk programmers can write more concise, flexible, and maintainable applications.

5.5 Control Structures: Using Blocks in Conditionals

Control structures are fundamental to any programming language, allowing developers to dictate the flow of execution based on certain conditions. In Smalltalk, blocks play a crucial role in creating flexible and powerful control structures, particularly conditionals. This section will discuss the use of block closures within conditional statements, including `ifTrue:`, `ifFalse:`, and `ifTrue:ifFalse:` messages.

A block closure in Smalltalk can be understood as an encapsulated chunk of code that can be evaluated at a later point. This characteristic makes blocks exceptionally useful in the construction of conditional statements.

Using ifTrue: and ifFalse: Messages

The simplest form of conditional in Smalltalk involves the `ifTrue:` and `ifFalse:` messages. These messages are sent to Boolean objects, and based on the Boolean value, either the block passed to `ifTrue:` or the block passed to `ifFalse:` is executed.

Consider the following example where a variable `$condition` holds a Boolean value:

```
condition
    ifTrue: [Transcript show: 'The condition is true.']
    ifFalse: [Transcript show: 'The condition is false.'].
```

In the above code, if `$condition` is `true`, the block passed to `ifTrue:` is executed, and "The condition is true." is printed in the Transcript. Conversely, if `$condition` is `false`, the block passed to `ifFalse:` is executed, printing "The condition is false."

Combining ifTrue: and ifFalse: with ifTrue:ifFalse:

Smalltalk also offers a more compact structure for conditionals using the `ifTrue:ifFalse:` message. This message expects two blocks as its arguments - the first block is executed if the receiver is `true`, and the second if the receiver is `false`.

Here is an example that demonstrates this:

```
condition
    ifTrue: [Transcript show: 'Executing true block.']
```

```
    ifFalse: [Transcript show: 'Executing false block.'].
```

This code achieves the same result as the previous example. The choice between using `ifTrue:ifFalse:` and separate `ifTrue:` and `ifFalse:` messages is often a matter of readability and preference.

Nesting Conditionals within Blocks

Blocks can be nested within other blocks, allowing for the creation of complex conditional logic. This nesting is particularly useful when dealing with multiple conditions that need to be evaluated consecutively or in combination.

Consider an example where we want to check two conditions:

```
condition1
    ifTrue: [condition2
            ifTrue: [Transcript show: 'Both conditions are true.']
            ifFalse: [Transcript show: 'Only condition1 is true.']]
    ifFalse: [Transcript show: 'Condition1 is false; not checking condition2.'].
```

In this nested structure, `condition2` is only evaluated if `condition1` is true, demonstrating how blocks can be used to build complex control flows.

Blocks are a powerful tool for implementing control structures in Smalltalk, especially conditionals. Their ability to encapsulate code for conditional execution allows for clearer, more concise code that adheres to the principles of modularity and reusability. As with all tools, the effectiveness of blocks in conditionals comes down to how they are used. Smalltalk programmers should strive to leverage blocks to create code that is not only functional but also easy to read and maintain.

5.6 Control Structures: Looping with Blocks

In this section, we will discuss the mechanism of looping within Smalltalk, focusing specifically on how blocks facilitate these iterations. Looping constructs in Smalltalk do not follow the conventional for or while syntax found in many other languages. Instead, looping is achieved through message passing to block closures, showcasing the language's commitment to object-oriented principles.

Basic Looping Constructs

Smalltalk provides several looping constructs, each designed to iterate over a sequence of instructions until a certain condition is met. Two of the most commonly used constructs are `whileTrue:` and `whileFalse:`. These messages are sent to blocks of code, and they control the execution flow based on the boolean result of another block.

Using whileTrue:

The `whileTrue:` message repeatedly executes a block of code as long as the condition block evaluates to true. Consider the following example, which prints numbers from 1 to 5:

```
| count |
count := 1.
[ count <= 5 ] whileTrue: [
    Transcript show: count printString; cr.
    count := count + 1.
].
```

In the above code, the variable `count` is initialized to 1. The block `[ count <= 5 ]` is our condition, and the block passed to `whileTrue:` contains the operations to be executed on each iteration. The `Transcript` is used to print the value of `count` to the Smalltalk Transcript window, followed by a carriage return (`cr`).

Using whileFalse:

Conversely, the `whileFalse:` message causes the block of code to execute as long as the condition block evaluates to false. The usage is similar to `whileTrue:`, but it serves the opposite purpose: to keep executing the block until the condition becomes false.

Iteration Over Collections

Smalltalk simplifies the iteration over collections by providing a rich set of messages that can be sent to collections, such as arrays, lists, and sets. Unlike explicit loop constructs, these methods abstract the iteration process, making the code shorter and more expressive.

Using do:

The `do:` message is sent to a collection, and it takes a block as an argument. Each element in the collection is passed to the block in succession. Here's how you can print each element in an array:

```
#(1 2 3 4 5) do: [:element |
    Transcript show: element printString; cr.
].
```

The array `#(1 2 3 4 5)` receives the `do:` message, with a block that receives each element (`:element`) and prints it. This pattern emphasizes the collection handling strength of Smalltalk, allowing operations on entire collections without explicit looping constructs.

Looping with Conditions and Collections

Combining conditional blocks and collection iteration provides a powerful mechanism for complex data processing. For instance, you can filter a collection based on a condition, then apply a operation to each remaining element, all within a compact and expressive syntax.

Example: Filtering and Processing

Consider we have an array of numbers and want to increment only the even numbers by 2, then print them:

```
| numbers |
numbers := #(2 3 4 5 6).
numbers select: [:each | each even] thenDo: [:each |
    | newNumber |
    newNumber := each + 2.
    Transcript show: newNumber printString; cr.
].
```

Here, `select:` is used to filter the elements, and `thenDo:` applies a block to each filtered element. Notice how the combination of these messages encapsulates a complex operation in a readable and concise way, a testament to Smalltalk's design principles focusing on simplicity and expressiveness.

Through the usage of blocks, Smalltalk's looping constructs depart from traditional imperative loops, offering a highly abstracted, object-oriented approach. This abstraction leads not only to greater code readability but also to enhanced expressiveness, allowing developers to write compact and flexible code for iteration and looping operations.

5.7 Using Blocks for Iteration over Collections

Smalltalk collections offer a rich interface for iteration, filtering, mapping, and reducing data. Blocks, as first-class citizens in Smalltalk, are the primary mechanism through which these operations are performed. This section will explore how to use blocks to iterate over collections, utilizing Smalltalk's powerful abstracted iteration patterns. These patterns not only reduce the boilerplate code but also enhance readability and maintainability.

Basic Iteration with `do:`

The `do:` method is one of the most fundamental iteration mechanisms provided by Smalltalk collections. It executes a given block for each element in the collection. The element under consideration is passed as an argument to the block.

```
#(1 2 3 4 5) do: [:each | Transcript show: each printString; cr].
```

In this example, for each element in the array, the element is printed to the Transcript. The block variable `:each` represents the current element from the collection being processed.

Collection Filtering with `select:` and `reject:`

Smalltalk provides high-level abstractions for filtering collections based on specific criteria. The `select:` method creates a new collection containing all elements that satisfy the condition defined in the passed block. Conversely, `reject:` includes those that do not satisfy the condition.

```
"| evenNumbers |"
evenNumbers := #(1 2 3 4 5 6) select: [:each | each even].
Transcript show: evenNumbers printString; cr. % Output: #(#2 #4 #6)

"| oddNumbers |"
oddNumbers := #(1 2 3 4 5 6) reject: [:each | each even].
Transcript show: oddNumbers printString; cr. % Output: #(#1 #3 #5)
```

These methods illustrate how blocks facilitate concise expression of collection processing logic, encapsulating conditional evaluations inside the block.

Mapping Collections with `collect:`

Mapping, or transforming collections, is accomplished with the `collect:` method. `collect:` applies a function, defined within a block, to each element of the collection, assembling a new collection with the results.

```
"| squaredNumbers |"
squaredNumbers := #(1 2 3 4 5) collect: [:each | each * each].
Transcript show: squaredNumbers printString; cr. % Output: #(#1 #4 #9 #16 #25)
```

This example demonstrates mapping each number to its square, showcasing the elegancy and power of expressive block syntax in iteration.

Iterating with Conditions: `detect:` and `detect:ifNone:`

The `detect:` method searches for the first element in a collection that satisfies the condition specified inside the block. The `detect:ifNone:` variant allows specifying a fallback action if no element meets the condition.

```
"| firstEvenNumber |"
firstEvenNumber := #(1 3 5 6 7) detect: [:each | each even] ifNone: [nil].
Transcript show: firstEvenNumber printString; cr. % Output: 6
```

This snippet illustrates searching for the first even number within an array, returning `nil` if there are no even numbers.

Reducing Collections with `inject:into:`

Reduction, or folding, is the process of combining the elements of a collection into a single value. The `inject:into:` method provides this functionality, where the first parameter is the initial accumulator value, and the block defines the reduction logic.

```
"| sum |"
sum := #(1 2 3 4 5) inject: 0 into: [:accumulator :each | accumulator + each].
Transcript show: sum printString; cr. % Output: 15
```

In this case, the sum of the numbers in the array is calculated by iteratively adding each element to an accumulator.

As demonstrated, Smalltalk's block closures provide a powerful and expressive mechanism for iterating over collections. By leveraging these high-level abstractions, developers can write cleaner, more maintainable code, adhering to the principles of compactness and functionality that define effective Smalltalk programming.

5.8 Exception Handling with Blocks

In handling exceptions, Smalltalk utilizes blocks to provide a framework for error recovery and management, ensuring programs can address unexpected conditions without crashing or producing incorrect results. Exception handling in Smalltalk is both elegant and powerful, allowing developers to encapsulate error-prone code within a block and define explicit recovery strategies.

To begin with, let's understand the syntax and structure for handling exceptions using blocks in Smalltalk. Exception handling is typically done using the `on:do:` method, where `on:` specifies the exception class to handle, and `do:` receives a block that defines the recovery strategy. Here is the basic form:

```
[ "Code that may raise an exception" ]
    on: ExceptionClass
    do: [:ex | "Recovery code"]
```

Here, `ExceptionClass` is the type of exception you are attempting to catch, and `ex` is the variable that will hold the exception object in the recovery block. This structure allows the program to continue running smoothly by handling errors gracefully.

For instance, consider a fragment of code that attempts to access an element by index from a list. If the index is out of bounds, an `Error` might occur. To handle this gracefully, we might use:

```
[ (myList at: 100) printString ]
    on: Error
    do: [:ex | 'Default value' printString].
```

In the example above, if accessing `myList` at index 100 causes an error (e.g., index out of bounds), the program will not crash. Instead, it prints a 'Default value' string, following the recovery strategy defined in the block passed to `do:`.

It's important to note that Smalltalk's exception handling mechanism allows for catching multiple exceptions, either by using different `on:do:` clauses for different exception classes or by using a hierarchy of exception classes in a single `on:do:` clause. This provides a versatile way to handle various error conditions with appropriate recovery strategies.

```
[ "Code prone to multiple types of exceptions" ]
    on: TypeOneException
    do: [:ex | "Recovery for TypeOneException"]
    on: TypeTwoException
    do: [:ex | "Recovery for TypeTwoException"].
```

Moreover, Smalltalk supports finally-like functionality through the `ensure:` method, which can follow the `on:do:` clauses. The block passed to `ensure:` executes regardless of whether an exception occurred, making it suitable for resource cleanup tasks:

```
[ "Code that might fail" ]
    on: ExceptionClass
    do: [:ex | "Handle exception"]
    ensure: [ "Cleanup code" ].
```

This structure ensures that, after attempting to execute the primary block and any necessary exception handling, the cleanup code will always run, thereby releasing resources or performing necessary finalization steps.

Exception handling with blocks in Smalltalk not only makes code more robust and error-resistant but does so in an expressive, clear manner. By leveraging blocks for both the potentially hazardous operation and its recovery strategy, Smalltalk programmers can compose elegant solutions that are easy to understand and maintain.

To conclude, mastering exception handling in Smalltalk through blocks is crucial for developing resilient applications. The approach allows for the detailed specification of behavior in the face of errors, which is an essential part of writing robust, reliable software.

5.9 Advanced Block Usage: Closures and Callbacks

Closures in Smalltalk are powerful constructs that encapsulate both a block of code and the environment in which they were created.

This makes them an indispensable tool for creating highly flexible and reusable code. In this section, we will delve into the more advanced uses of closures, focusing on their role in implementing callbacks and the benefits they offer in various programming scenarios.

First, let's explore the concept of a callback function. A callback function is a piece of executable code that is passed as an argument to another piece of code, which is expected to execute the callback at a certain time. This programming technique allows for a high degree of modularity and abstraction, enabling asynchronous or event-driven programming.

```
"Defining a simple closure"
| myClosure |
myClosure := [ :x | x squared ].
```

In the example above, `myClosure` is a block closure that takes a single argument, `x`, and returns its square. This closure can be used as a callback for various operations.

```
"Using the closure as a callback with a collection"
(1 to: 5) collect: myClosure.
```

The code snippet illustrates the use of `myClosure` as a callback function with the `collect:` method, which applies the closure to each element in the collection (1 to 5), resulting in a new collection of squared values.

```
Output: #(1 4 9 16 25)
```

The concept of closures becomes particularly valuable when dealing with asynchronous operations or tasks that may not complete immediately. For instance, in event-driven programming, a particular action or event may trigger the execution of a closure.

Another advanced application of closures is in the creation of custom control structures. Smalltalk allows programmers to define their own control structures using blocks, offering a level of expressiveness and flexibility not readily available in many other languages.

```
"Defining a custom control structure"
| collection conditionBlock |
```

```
collection := 1 to: 10.
conditionBlock := [ :element | element even ].
collection select: conditionBlock.
```

In the above example, `conditionBlock` is a closure that checks if a given element is even. The `select:` method then uses this closure to filter elements in `collection`, returning only those that satisfy the condition specified by `conditionBlock`.

```
Output: #(2 4 6 8 10)
```

Finally, closures can be effectively utilized for error handling and exception management. By wrapping a potentially error-prone block of code in a closure, developers can define custom handlers for exceptions, making their programs more robust and resilient.

In summary, the use of closures and callbacks in Smalltalk significantly enhances the language's expressiveness and the programmer's ability to write concise, flexible, and reusable code. This chapter segment has showcased the power of closures in various advanced programming contexts, including asynchronous calls, custom control structures, and error handling, illuminating the elegance and versatility that make Smalltalk an enduringly valuable tool in the software developer's arsenal.

5.10 Performance Considerations with Blocks

In this section, we will discuss performance considerations associated with the use of blocks in Smalltalk. While blocks offer a powerful and expressive means to encapsulate behavior and control program flow, it is crucial to be mindful of their impact on the application's runtime efficiency. The primary aspects to consider are memory usage, execution time, and the potential for creating retain cycles in certain contexts.

Memory Usage

Blocks in Smalltalk are objects, and like any object, they consume memory. However, their memory usage is not only attributed to the block itself but also to the context in which they are defined. This is because blocks capture their surrounding context, holding references to variables and objects that are accessible within their scope.

- When a block is created, it captures and retains a snapshot of its lexical environment. This means all variables accessible in the block's scope at the time of its creation are retained in memory, potentially increasing the memory footprint of your application.

- The memory overhead for each block is generally small, but in applications where large numbers of blocks are created or blocks capture large objects, this overhead can accumulate, leading to noticeable increases in memory usage.

Execution Time

The execution time of blocks can vary significantly based on their complexity and the operations they perform. However, two primary factors affect the performance of blocks from an execution standpoint:

- The process of creating a block, capturing its context, and allocating memory for it entails a certain amount of overhead. While minimal for individual blocks, this overhead can become significant in situations where many blocks are created, such as in tight loops or recursive functions.

- Blocks that capture a large context or perform complex computations can take longer to execute, directly impacting the performance of the application.

Retain Cycles

One of the subtler aspects of using blocks that can affect performance is the creation of retain cycles. This occurs when a block captures a reference to an object that, in turn, maintains a reference to the block, creating a cycle that prevents the objects involved from being deallocated.

- Retain cycles are particularly problematic in long-lived objects or those that consume substantial resources. They can lead to memory leaks, whereby objects remain in memory even after they are no longer needed, reducing the available memory for other parts of the application.
- Avoiding retain cycles requires careful management of references within blocks. This often involves using 'weak references' for objects that the block captures, ensuring that these objects are not strongly retained by the block and can be properly deallocated.

Optimization Strategies

The performance implications of using blocks in Smalltalk necessitate employing strategies to optimize their use. Some key strategies include:

- Minimizing the context that blocks capture by only accessing the variables and objects necessary for their execution. This reduces the memory overhead and the potential for retain cycles.
- Using blocks judiciously, especially in performance-critical parts of the application. Consider alternatives such as direct method invocations when blocks are not essential for abstraction or control flow.
- Profiling and analyzing the application to identify bottlenecks related to block usage. Tools and techniques specific to Smalltalk environments can assist in pinpointing where optimization efforts should be focused.

In summary, while blocks are a powerful tool in the Smalltalk programmer's arsenal, understanding and mitigating their potential performance impacts is crucial for developing efficient and responsive applications.

5.11 Debugging Techniques for Blocks

Debugging in Smalltalk, particularly within block closures, is both an art and a science. Given their encapsulation of actions as first-class objects, blocks offer flexibility but can also present unique challenges when identifying and resolving issues. This section will discuss several effective strategies for debugging blocks, focusing on identifying common pitfalls, inspecting block states, and utilizing debugging tools within the Smalltalk environment.

First, it's crucial to understand the common issues that arise with blocks. These can range from scope-related errors, where variables are not accessible within the block, to logical errors resulting from unexpected block execution sequences. To mitigate these issues, developers should:

- Ensure that all variables used inside a block are correctly scoped. This involves understanding the distinction between global, instance, and local variables in the context of block execution.
- Pay close attention to the execution flow, particularly in blocks passed as arguments to higher-order functions or used in control structures. Incorrect assumptions about when a block is executed can lead to challenging bugs.

To inspect the state of a block during debugging, Smalltalk's reflective capabilities are invaluable. Reflective programming in Smalltalk allows developers to inspect, modify, and dynamically interact with the program during its execution. This can be particularly useful for examining the state of variables within a block. Here is an example of how one might programmatically inspect a block's state:

```
| myBlock localVar |
localVar := 10.
myBlock := [ :x | x + localVar ].
Transcript show: (myBlock value: 5) printString; cr.
```

In this example, we define a block that takes a parameter and adds it to a local variable. By using Smalltalk's `Transcript`, we can print the result of executing the block with a specific argument. During debugging, similar techniques can be employed to inspect or modify block internals.

Smalltalk provides several tools and utilities aimed at simplifying the debugging process. Among the most powerful is the built-in debugger, which allows step-by-step execution of code, including block closures. To effectively use the debugger with blocks, follow these steps:

- When an error occurs, Smalltalk's environment will automatically prompt you with the debugger window.
- Navigate to the context in which the block was defined or executed. This may involve stepping through higher-order function calls or iterating over collection-processing methods.
- Once within the desired context, you can step into the block's execution. This allows you to see the values of variables at each step and the flow of execution within the block.

Performance considerations are important when debugging blocks, especially in computational heavy or real-time applications. The act of debugging itself can introduce additional overhead. Therefore, judicious use of debugging statements, like `Transcript` output, is advised. Moreover, profiling tools available within Smalltalk can help identify performance bottlenecks attributed to block execution, enabling targeted optimizations.

Finally, embracing best practices during blocks development can preemptively reduce debugging efforts. These include:

- Writing small, focused blocks that accomplish a single task.

- Employing clear naming conventions for blocks and variables, enhancing readability and making code behavior more predictable.
- Modularizing code by leveraging blocks, which can simplify both testing and debugging by isolating functionality.

Debugging block closures in Smalltalk involves a combination of understanding common pitfalls, leveraging the language's reflective capabilities, and utilizing built-in tools and strategies for effective debugging. By adhering to best practices and employing a methodical approach to diagnosing and resolving issues, developers can navigate the complexities of block debugging and ensure the robustness of their Smalltalk applications.

5.12 Best Practices for Writing Clean and Efficient Blocks

In adhering to best practices for writing clean and efficient blocks in Smalltalk, the core principles revolve around clarity, maintainability, and performance efficiency. Blocks, being a fundamental construct in Smalltalk, offer tremendous flexibility but also require a disciplined approach to ensure code quality. This section outlines several guidelines to optimize block usage.

- **Minimize Block Size**: Blocks should be kept concise and focused on a single task. Larger blocks can become difficult to read and maintain, obscuring the underlying logic. If a block grows too large, consider breaking it down into smaller blocks or private methods within the class.
- **Clear Variable Naming**: The variables within blocks, including parameters and temporaries, should have clear, descriptive names. This enhances readability and makes the block's purpose and functionality evident at a glance.

```
[ :x | | squared |
```

```
    squared := x * x.
    squared ].
```

This example demonstrates a block that calculates the square of a number, with clearly named variables for easy understanding.

- **Avoid Side Effects**: Blocks should be designed to avoid side effects where possible. A side effect is any state change that occurs outside of the block's scope, making the code more difficult to follow and predict. Pure functions, which depend only on their inputs and produce no side effects, are preferable within blocks.

- **Limit Scope of Variables**: The scope of variables used within a block should be as narrow as possible. This minimizes the block's dependencies and makes it more portable and reusable. It also reduces the risk of unintended interactions with other parts of the code.

- **Use Blocks for Abstraction**: Leverage blocks to encapsulate complex logic or control structures, making the outer code more elegant and readable. This not only improves maintainability but also emphasizes the power of blocks for creating higher-order functions.

```
numbers select: [ :n | n odd ].
```

Here, the `select:` method demonstrates using a block to abstract away the details of filtering a collection for odd numbers.

- **Performance Considerations**: While blocks enhance readability and abstraction, be mindful of their impact on performance, especially in tight loops or critical sections of code. Evaluate the necessity of blocks in such contexts and consider alternative approaches if a significant performance penalty is observed.

- **Debugging Blocks**: Debugging issues within blocks can be challenging due to their anonymous nature and the potential for deferred execution. Incorporate logging or breakpoints within blocks to aid in tracing and debugging efforts.

- **Commenting and Documentation**: Although blocks can make code more readable, complex logic within blocks should be accompanied by comments that explain the block's purpose and any non-obvious details of its implementation.

```
[ :x | "Calculates the square of x"
   x * x ].
```

  Effective commenting aids in the maintainability of block-intensive code, especially for complex algorithms or business logic.

- **Consistent Styling**: Adhering to a consistent coding style, including indentation, spacing, and bracket use, improves the readability of blocks. Team or project-specific style guides should be followed to ensure uniformity across the codebase.

Adopting these best practices not only improves the quality and efficiency of Smalltalk blocks but also contributes to the overall maintainability and elegance of the code. Blocks are a powerful feature of Smalltalk, offering significant flexibility in how code is structured and executed. By following these guidelines, developers can harness this power effectively, crafting clean, efficient, and readable block-based constructs.

Chapter 6

Error Handling and Debugging in Smalltalk

Effective error handling and debugging are critical components of software development, ensuring the reliability and robustness of applications. Smalltalk provides a comprehensive set of tools and constructs for dealing with exceptions, signaling errors, and debugging code. This chapter introduces the frameworks and techniques for managing errors and debugging in Smalltalk, covering exception handling mechanisms, the use of the integrated development environment (IDE) for debugging, and best practices for identifying and resolving issues in code. By mastering these skills, readers will be equipped to maintain high-quality, error-free Smalltalk applications.

6.1 Overview of Error Handling in Smalltalk

Error handling is an indispensable aspect of software development, enabling applications to manage and respond to unforeseen issues during runtime. Smalltalk, with its rich development environment, provides a robust framework for handling errors, ensuring applications can recover gracefully from unexpected situations.

The cornerstone of error handling in Smalltalk is the exception model, which is built on the foundation of objects and messages. Unlike procedural programming languages where error handling may be achieved through error codes and global flags, Smalltalk uses its inherent object-oriented paradigm to manage errors as objects. These error objects can carry detailed information about the error, such as the error type, message, and the stack trace at the point the error occurred. This object-oriented approach not only makes error handling more intuitive but also significantly more flexible.

Smalltalk categorizes errors into two main types: exceptions and signals.

- **Exceptions** are typically used to indicate that something has gone wrong in the program. They are objects that are instances of the class `Exception` or one of its subclasses. Exceptions are meant to be caught and handled by the code that can recover from the error situation.

- **Signals**, meanwhile, are a kind of control flow mechanism. They are also objects (instances of the class `Signal` or its subclasses) and are used for controlling program flow based on certain conditions, not necessarily when something goes wrong. Signals can be handled in a manner similar to exceptions, but they are often used in scenarios where normal control structures would not suffice.

Handling errors effectively in Smalltalk involves several key activities:

1. **Raising an exception or signal:** This is where an error or a specific condition is encountered, and an exception or signal object is created and 'thrown' to indicate that a special situation has occurred.

2. **Catching and handling the exception or signal:** This involves intercepting the raised exception or signal and executing specific code to manage or recover from the situation.

3. **Propagating the exception:** If an exception cannot be handled where it is caught, it may be necessary to propagate it further up the call stack, to be caught and handled by another part of the program.

Smalltalk's error handling mechanism provides great flexibility and power to developers, enabling them to write resilient and robust applications. By leveraging the capabilities of the Smalltalk environment and its object-oriented model, developers can effectively manage errors and exceptions, leading to higher-quality, reliable software. Understanding the nuances of Smalltalk's error handling approach is therefore crucial for mastering the language and developing proficient Smalltalk applications.

6.2 Understanding Smalltalk Exceptions and Signals

In this section, we will discuss the fundamental concepts of exceptions and signals within Smalltalk. Understanding these elements is essential for efficient error handling and debugging in your applications.

Smalltalk's approach to exceptions is similar to that seen in many object-oriented programming languages, where exceptions are used to handle unforeseen errors during runtime. However, Smalltalk adds a unique spin with its signal mechanism, which allows for more granular control over error handling.

Exception Handling Basics

In Smalltalk, an exception is an object that represents an error or an unusual event in the program. When such an event occurs, an exception is `raised` or `signaled`, interrupting the normal flow of the program.

The syntax for raising an exception in Smalltalk is straightforward. The `Exception new signal` method can be used to raise a generic exception. However, Smalltalk encourages the use of more specific exception classes to convey clearer information about the error that has occurred.

```
ZeroDivide new signal: 'Attempt to divide by zero.'
```

This code snippet raises a `ZeroDivide` exception with a message indicating that a division by zero was attempted.

Signals in Smalltalk

Signals in Smalltalk are similar to exceptions but are typically used for control flow rather than error handling. A signal is an instance of `Signal` or any subclass thereof. When a signal is raised, it traverses up the call stack searching for a matching `handler`. If no handler is found, it will proceed as an unhandled exception.

Raising a signal uses a syntax similar to exceptions:

```
(MyCustomSignal new) signal.
```

Here, `MyCustomSignal` represents a custom signal class that you might define in your application.

Handling Exceptions and Signals

To handle exceptions or signals in Smalltalk, the program must include `exception blocks` or `signal handlers`. These blocks are defined using the `on:do:` message, which takes a class (the exception or signal to catch) and a block of code (the handler to execute).

```
[1 / 0] on: ZeroDivide do: [:ex | Transcript show: ex messageText; cr].
```

In this example, an attempt to divide by zero is encapsulated within a try block. The `on:do:` message specifies that in the case of a

`ZeroDivide` exception, a block should be executed that prints the exception's message to the Transcript.

Best Practices

In designing applications, it is recommended to use specific exceptions and signals for different error conditions. This granularity allows for more precise error handling and makes the program more comprehensible and maintainable.

Furthermore, while it may be tempting to use signals for controlling application flow, it is generally advisable to reserve signals for exceptional conditions or events out of the ordinary flow. Overusing signals for regular control flow can make the code less readable and harder to debug.

Understanding how to effectively use exceptions and signals is crucial for developing robust Smalltalk applications. By raising specific exceptions in error conditions and handling them gracefully, you can ensure that your applications are resilient against unforeseen errors and provide a better user experience.

In the next section, we will delve into the specifics of raising and catching exceptions in Smalltalk, providing code examples and best practices to enhance your error handling strategies.

6.3 Raising and Catching Exceptions

Raising and catching exceptions are fundamental operations in handling errors within Smalltalk programs. This mechanism allows programs to respond to unexpected events or conditions gracefully, without crashing or producing incorrect results.

Raising Exceptions

In Smalltalk, an exception is raised by sending the message `signal` to an instance of the `Error` class or one of its subclasses. This action interrupts the normal flow of execution and begins the search for an appropriate exception handler.

Let's illustrate how to raise a generic exception:

```
Error new signal: 'An unexpected error occurred.'
```

However, it's often more useful to raise specific types of exceptions. Smalltalk's standard library provides a variety of built-in exception classes that represent different error conditions. For example, to indicate a division by zero, one could use:

```
ZeroDivide new signal.
```

Catching Exceptions

After an exception is raised, it's important to catch and handle it appropriately to prevent it from crashing the program. In Smalltalk, this is done using the `on:do:` method. This method takes two arguments: the exception class to catch and a block of code to execute when the exception is caught.

Here is a simple example of catching an exception:

```
[1 / 0] on: ZeroDivide do: [:ex |
    Transcript show: 'Caught a division by zero!'; cr.
].
```

In this example, the division by zero would typically raise a `ZeroDivide` exception, disrupting the normal flow. However, the `on:do:` method catches this specific type of exception and executes a block that prints a message to the Transcript, thus handling the error.

Combining Raising and Catching Exceptions

Combining the mechanisms for raising and catching exceptions allows developers to write robust and error-resistant programs. When an exceptional condition is detected, an error can be signaled, and the surrounding code can catch and handle this error gracefully.

Consider the following example where custom error checking and handling are implemented:

```
["Custom code that might fail" on: CustomError do: [:ex |
   Transcript show: 'Handling custom error'; cr.
]] on: Error do: [:ex |
   Transcript show: 'An unexpected error occurred'; cr.
].
```

In this composite structure, a potentially failing piece of code is wrapped in an `on:do:` block tailored for a custom error. Additionally, this entire construct is enclosed in another `on:do:` block designed to catch any unexpected errors that weren't explicitly accounted for, providing a layered approach to error handling.

It is essential to use exception handling judiciously to maintain the clarity and maintainability of the codebase. Overuse or misuse of exceptions can lead to programs that are difficult to understand and debug.

6.4 Creating Custom Exceptions

Creating custom exceptions in Smalltalk not only aids in making error handling more intuitive and maintainable but also allows for the encapsulation of error-specific information, which can be immensely useful for debugging and error logging. Smalltalk's flexible and dynamic nature makes it straightforward to define custom exceptions that cater to the unique needs of an application. In this section, we will explore the steps involved in creating and utilizing custom exceptions, adhering to best practices.

In Smalltalk, exceptions are objects, and defining a custom exception involves creating a new class that inherits from the `Exception` class or one of its subclasses. This inheritance is crucial because it ensures that the custom exception inherits the behavior essential for participating in Smalltalk's exception handling mechanisms.

Let's start with the skeleton of a custom exception class:

```
Object subclass: #MyCustomException
```

```
    instanceVariableNames: ''
    classVariableNames: ''
    poolDictionaries: ''
    category: 'MyApplication-Errors'.
```

This code snippet demonstrates the creation of a new class `MyCustomException` that directly inherits from `Object`. For an exception, however, it's more appropriate to inherit from `Exception` or one of its specific subclasses to gain the necessary exception handling behavior.

```
Exception subclass: #MyCustomException
    instanceVariableNames: 'additionalInfo'
    classVariableNames: ''
    poolDictionaries: ''
    category: 'MyApplication-Errors'.
```

In this revised definition, `MyCustomException` correctly inherits from `Exception` and includes an instance variable named `additionalInfo`. This variable is intended to store any supplementary information relevant to the exception, enhancing the error reporting capabilities.

To effectively utilize this custom exception, it's beneficial to implement a method that initializes the exception object with custom data. Here is an example:

```
MyCustomException >> initializeWithInfo: anInfo
    super initialize.
    additionalInfo := anInfo.
```

This method, `initializeWithInfo:`, is responsible for setting up the exception instance by invoking the superclass `initialize` method to ensure proper initialization and then storing the provided information in the `additionalInfo` instance variable.

Raising the custom exception within application code can be accomplished as follows:

```
MyCustomException signal: 'An error occurred' withInfo: 'DetailedInformation'.
```

Here, the custom exception is signaled (or thrown) using the `signal:withInfo:` method, which leverages the previously defined `initializeWithInfo:` method to pass along a descriptive message and additional details about the error.

Creating custom exceptions in Smalltalk involves subclassing `Exception` or one of its descendants, potentially adding instance variables for storing additional error information, and defining initialization methods for properly setting up the exception object. Custom exceptions enhance the ability to handle errors gracefully, providing a mechanism to encapsulate and convey extensive error information, which significantly aids in debugging and error resolution processes.

6.5 Best Practices for Exception Handling

In this section, we will discuss the fundamental best practices for exception handling in Smalltalk, which enhance code reliability and maintainability. Exception handling, if not executed properly, can lead to code that is difficult to read, maintain, or debug. Applying these best practices ensures that your applications are robust and error-resistant.

The first principle to understand is the importance of precise exception capturing. Catching exceptions more broadly than necessary can obscure the source of an error, making debugging more challenging. Therefore, it's crucial to catch specific exceptions rather than resorting to a catch-all approach.

```
"Example of precise exception handling"
[ aCollection doSomething ]
   on: SpecificException
   do: [ :ex | "Handle the specific exception" ].
```

This code snippet demonstrates handling a `SpecificException`, ensuring that only errors of this type are caught and processed accordingly.

Another best practice is to ensure that resources are properly managed, even when exceptions occur. This is often referred to as guaranteed resource cleanup. In Smalltalk, the `ensure:` block is used to execute code that must run regardless of whether an exception is thrown.

```
"Example of guaranteed resource cleanup"
[ aResource allocate.
  aResource useThatMayThrowAnException. ]
    ensure: [ aResource deallocate. ].
```

In this example, the `ensure:` block guarantees that `aResource` is deallocated, thus avoiding resource leaks even if an exception interrupts the normal flow of execution.

Implementing custom exceptions is another effective strategy. Custom exceptions allow developers to convey more context about the error, facilitating quicker diagnosis and resolution. The creation of a custom exception in Smalltalk is straightforward, typically involving subclassing `Exception`.

```
Exception subclass: #MyCustomException
    instanceVariableNames: ''
    classVariableNames: ''
    poolDictionaries: ''
    category: 'MyApplication-Errors'.
```

This code defines a `MyCustomException`, which can then be thrown and caught specifically, providing more detailed error information.

Logging exceptions is another critical practice. Detailed logs can significantly aid in diagnosing issues, especially when reproducing the error is difficult. Logging should include as much context as possible, such as the time of the exception, the stack trace, and any relevant application state.

```
"Example of exception logging"
[ aCollection doSomethingRisky ]
    on: Error
    do: [ :ex |
        Transcript show: 'Error occurred at: ', Time now printString; cr.
        Transcript show: 'With exception: ', ex printString; cr.
        ex pass. ].
```

In this example, upon encountering an error, details about the error and the time it occurred are logged using the `Transcript`.

Last but not least, avoid using exceptions for flow control. Exceptions should represent unexpected events or error conditions, not regular control flow mechanisms.

To sum up, adopting these best practices for exception handling in Smalltalk not only makes your code more robust and error-tolerant but also significantly more maintainable and easier to debug. Precise exception capturing, resource cleanup guarantees, the use of custom exceptions, diligent logging, and proper use of exceptions contribute greatly to the resilience of Smalltalk applications.

6.6 Using the Debugger: Basics and Navigation

Smalltalk's integrated development environment (IDE) includes a powerful debugging tool that significantly simplifies the process of identifying and correcting errors. This debugger provides an interactive interface, enabling developers to examine the state of the program at the time of an exception or a breakpoint. Let's discuss the foundational knowledge required to effectively navigate and utilize the Smalltalk debugger.

Opening the Debugger

To initiate the debugger in Smalltalk, an error must occur during the execution of your program, or a breakpoint must be reached. Alternatively, you can manually trigger the debugger by sending the `halt` message to any object.

```
"Manually invoking the debugger"
Transcript show: 'About to halt.'; cr.
self halt.
Transcript show: 'This line will not execute until debugger resumes.'; cr.
```

Upon execution of the `halt` message, the debugger window opens, showing the context in which the halt occurred.

Navigating the Debugger Interface

The debugger interface is divided into several key areas:

- The upper pane displays the call stack — a list of all active method calls at the point where the debugger was opened.
- The middle pane shows the source code of the currently selected method in the call stack.
- The lower pane displays the variables (instance, temporary, and parameters) and their current values in the selected method context.

To inspect the flow of execution leading up to the breakpoint or error, one should navigate through the call stack by clicking on the method entries. This allows the examination of the state of the program at various execution points.

Stepping Through Code

The debugger provides several stepping operations, enabling fine-grained control over program execution:

- `Step Over` executes the current line of code, including any method calls, without entering those methods in the debugger.
- `Step Into` executes the current method call, opening a new context in the debugger if the method is defined in the source code.
- `Step Out` continues execution until the current method returns, useful for exiting the current context.

Here is an example of stepping through code:

```
"Example method invoking another method"
exampleMethod
    Transcript show: 'In exampleMethod'; cr.
    self anotherMethod.

"Method called within exampleMethod"
anotherMethod
    Transcript show: 'In anotherMethod'; cr.
```

By using `Step Into` on the call to `self anotherMethod`, the debugger will move into the `anotherMethod` context.

Inspecting Variables

To inspect the value of a variable in the debugger:

1. Select the method in the call stack where the variable is defined or accessible.

2. Locate the variable in the lower pane.

3. The current value of the variable will be shown alongside its name.

This feature is crucial for understanding the state of the program and diagnosing issues related to variable values.

Setting and Removing Breakpoints

While the `halt` message is useful for debugging, Smalltalk also allows setting breakpoints directly in the source code through the IDE, which can then be enabled or disabled as required. To set a breakpoint, right-click on a line number in the editor and select the option to insert a breakpoint. Similarly, removing a breakpoint is done by right-clicking on the breakpoint indicator and choosing to remove it.

Navigating and using the Smalltalk debugger is a skill that improves with practice. Familiarity with these basics will enhance your ability to quickly and effectively resolve issues in your Smalltalk applications, leading to more reliable and robust software.

6.7 Setting Breakpoints and Inspecting Variables

Effective debugging in Smalltalk largely hinges on the developer's capacity to judiciously set breakpoints and meticulously inspect the state of variables at various execution points. Breakpoints serve as intentional pausing spots in a program's execution, facilitating the examination of the program's behavior and state. This section elucidates the methodology for setting breakpoints and inspecting variables within the context of the Smalltalk integrated development environment (IDE).

Setting Breakpoints

To set a breakpoint in Smalltalk, one employs the method `halt`. Inserting this method into the code instructs the Smalltalk environment to pause execution at that juncture, thereby invoking the debugger. The syntax for inserting a breakpoint is straightforward:

```
methodName
    "code before breakpoint"
    self halt.
    "code after breakpoint"
```

Upon reaching the `halt` method during execution, Smalltalk opens the debugger interface, displaying the current class and method, along with the stack trace and variable states at the time of the pause.

It is noteworthy that judicious placement of breakpoints is crucial. A well-placed breakpoint can illuminate the cause of an error or undesirable program behavior, but excessive or poorly positioned breakpoints may obfuscate the issue by breaking the flow of execution too frequently or in irrelevant locations.

Inspecting Variables

Once a breakpoint halts program execution, inspecting variables is essential to understand the program's current state. Smalltalk's IDE provides two primary means for variable inspection: through the debugger interface and using the `inspect` method in code.

Debugger Interface: Within the debugger, variables in scope at the breakpoint pause are displayed. Selecting a variable from this list presents its current value. For objects, the IDE shows the object's instance variables and their values, facilitating a deep dive into the object's current state. This graphical inspection is intuitive and does not require additional code.

Using the `inspect` Method: For a more targeted inspection, the `inspect` method can be strategically placed in the code, similar to setting a breakpoint. This method opens an inspector window for any object it is called on, enabling the examination of that object's state. The usage is as follows:

```
anObject inspect.
```

Here, `anObject` is the variable you wish to inspect. Upon execution reaching this line, an inspector window for `anObject` will open, revealing its internals without halting the program, unlike `halt`.

Combining breakpoints with variable inspection offers a powerful mechanism for diagnosing and rectifying issues within Smalltalk applications. By pausing the execution at critical points and examining the state of the application through its variables, developers can gain insightful perspectives on the source of errors or unexpected behavior, thereby streamlining the debugging process.

6.8 Step Execution and Call Stack Analysis

In this section, we will discuss step execution and call stack analysis, two fundamental practices for debugging in Smalltalk. The ability to step through code execution line by line and examine the call stack is invaluable for understanding program flow and identifying errors.

Step Execution

Step execution, or single-stepping, is the process of executing a program one instruction at a time. This permits the programmer to observe the changing state of the application at each step. Smalltalk's integrated development environment (IDE) provides tools for step execution, facilitating a granular inspection of the program's behavior.

To initiate step execution in Smalltalk, one would typically use the debugging tools available in the IDE. Here's an example:

```
Transcript show: 'Starting step execution.'.
factorial := 1.
1 to: 5 do: [:n |
   factorial := factorial * n.
   Transcript show: 'Factorial of ', n printString, ' is ', factorial
        printString.
].
Transcript show: 'Finished.'.
```

By setting a breakpoint at the beginning of this block of code, a programmer can step through each operation. At each step, Smalltalk's IDE allows observation of variable values, which is crucial for verifying the correctness of the program logic.

Call Stack Analysis

The call stack is a record of active subroutines or functions in a program's execution history. Analyzing the call stack is especially useful in the context of exceptions or errors. It allows developers to trace the sequence of calls that led to the problematic state.

Smalltalk provides a call stack tool within its debugging environment, enabling developers to navigate through the sequence of method invocations. An example of using the call stack might involve an unexpected error occurring during program execution. By examining the call stack, the developer can identify the origin of the error.

The graphical representation of the call stack typically includes:

- The name of each method in the call sequence.
- The line number where the method was called.
- The current values of variables at each level of the stack.

Combining step execution with call stack analysis offers a powerful approach to debugging. While step execution allows for close observation of program behavior one line at a time, call stack analysis provides a macro view of the sequence of method invocations leading to the current point in the program.

To illustrate, consider the following code snippet:

```
someMethod
    ^self performCalculation.

performCalculation
    ^1 / 0.
```

If 'someMethod' is called, Smalltalk's debugger will interrupt execution when the division by zero occurs in 'performCalculation'. At this point, examining the call stack will reveal that 'performCalculation' was invoked by 'someMethod', thereby helping identify the flow that led to the error.

Practical Applications

Effective use of step execution and call stack analysis can drastically reduce the time required to identify and fix bugs in a Smalltalk application. Developers are encouraged to:

- Regularly use step execution when testing new code to validate logic and ensure correct behavior.
- Utilize call stack analysis when confronted with errors or exceptions to quickly pinpoint the source of problems.

Mastering step execution and call stack analysis equips Smalltalk developers with vital debugging skills, enhancing their ability to maintain and improve application quality.

6.9 Performance Profiling and Optimization Tools

In software development, particularly within Smalltalk environments, understanding and enhancing the performance of the application is paramount. Performance profiling and optimization tools are indispensable in identifying bottlenecks, understanding how code changes impact performance, and pinpointing areas that require optimization. Smalltalk offers a range of tools geared towards facilitating these tasks efficiently.

One primary tool for performance profiling in Smalltalk is the `MessageTally` class. `MessageTally` is used to collect and report statistics on message sends (method invocations) within the application, providing insights into which parts of the code are the most time-consuming. To use `MessageTally` for profiling an execution block, the following syntax is employed:

```
MessageTally spyOn: [YourCodeBlockHere].
```

The output from `MessageTally` is comprehensive, offering a hierarchical breakdown of time spent in each method. This allows developers to swiftly identify methods that are significant performance consumers and thus candidates for optimization.

Another useful feature is the `TimeProfileBrowser`, which offers a graphical interface for examining the profiling data collected by `MessageTally`. It provides an intuitive means of navigating through method calls and understanding their performance implications in a visual manner.

```
- YourApplication>MainClass>yourMethod        25ms
  - YourApplication>SubClass>anotherMethod    15ms
    - String>do:                              10ms
```

For optimizing database interactions, which are often performance-critical, Smalltalk provides the `DBMonitor` tool. `DBMonitor` assists in identifying and analyzing database queries that are inefficient or unnecessarily complex, allowing for targeted optimizations.

In addition to tooling specific for performance analysis, Smalltalk's integrated development environment (IDE) supports various features that aid in the optimization process. For instance, the Refactoring Browser enables developers to safely modify and improve the structure of code without changing its behavior, a common requirement during optimization efforts.

When considering memory usage, which is intrinsically tied to performance, Smalltalk offers garbage collection analysis tools. These tools help identify memory leaks and optimize memory usage patterns, ensuring that applications use resources efficiently and maintain performance over time.

For code that is particularly performance-sensitive, Smalltalk also supports inline C code through its Foreign Function Interface (FFI). This offers a path to optimizing critical sections of code by harnessing the speed of C, directly from within Smalltalk. An example of using FFI for performance reasons might be:

```
FFI call: #(int "externalLibraryFunction" (int)).
```

Lastly, it is important to utilize the `SystemReporter` tool to obtain a comprehensive report on the overall system's state and performance. This includes information on memory usage, garbage collection statistics, and idle time. This report can provide a high-level overview of performance and is especially useful for identifying systemic issues.

- Collect method invocation statistics with `MessageTally`.

- Navigate profiling data using the `TimeProfileBrowser`.
- Identify inefficient database queries with `DBMonitor`.
- Use Refactoring Browser for safe code optimization.
- Analyze memory usage and optimize with garbage collection analysis tools.
- Leverage the power of C for critical performance sections via FFI.
- Obtain a comprehensive system performance report with `SystemReporter`.

By leveraging these tools, Smalltalk developers can not only identify performance bottlenecks but also apply precise optimizations to improve application responsiveness and efficiency. This becomes increasingly critical as applications grow in complexity and size, necessitating a systematic approach to performance management.

6.10 Tips for Efficient Debugging Strategies

In the domain of software development, debugging is an inevitable and essential process. An efficient debugging strategy not only aids in identifying and correcting errors but also enhances the developer's understanding of the software's operational dynamics. This section delineates several strategies to augment the efficacy of debugging efforts in Smalltalk programming.

Firstly, it's imperative to adopt a methodical approach to debugging. Instead of haphazardly examining code snippets where the bug is presumed to exist, developers should:

- Rigorously examine the error message or abnormal behavior to understand the issue's context.
- Trace the execution flow to pinpoint the source of the error.

- Break down the problem, isolating the components involved to localize the root cause.

Implementing a divide-and-conquer strategy can dramatically simplify the debugging process. By partitioning the application into smaller, testable units, developers can identify faulty segments more efficiently. This technique aligns well with Smalltalk's object-oriented paradigm, allowing each object to be inspected independently.

Another critical strategy involves leveraging the logging capability provided by Smalltalk. Strategic placement of logging statements can yield insights into the application's execution flow and state at various points, aiding in pinpointing discrepancies. A simplistic example of logging within Smalltalk is shown below:

```
Transcript show: 'Debugging Step: Entering method X with value: ', aVariable
    printString; cr.
```

The `Transcript` window acts as a console, displaying runtime information that can be invaluable during debugging.

Further, the utilization of version control systems plays a pivotal role. By committing changes incrementally, developers can compare versions to identify which modifications introduced the bug. This practice not only streamlines the process of isolating issues but also encourages smaller, manageable commits that are easier to review and debug.

Moreover, peer review of code should not be underestimated. Fresh eyes can often spot oversights that the original developer may miss. In Smalltalk, leveraging pair programming or conducting code reviews with fellow developers can provide new perspectives and insights, contributing to more effective debugging.

Regarding tooling, Smalltalk's integrated development environment (IDE) offers powerful debugging tools. Familiarity with these tools and their capabilities can significantly expedite the debugging process. Techniques include:

- Setting breakpoints to pause execution and inspect the current state.

- Stepping through code line by line to observe behavior and variable states.
- Utilizing the call stack to trace method invocations and their origins.

To encapsulate, here are general guidelines to enhance debugging efficacy:

- Understand the problem thoroughly before attempting to debug.
- Isolate and minimize the code base to the smallest subset that reproduces the error.
- Use the IDE's debugging tools to their full extent, familiarizing oneself with shortcuts and features.
- Maintain a disciplined approach to version control, ensuring easy access to historical states of the application.
- Engage in peer review to leverage different perspectives and insights.

Debugging is as much an art as it is a science. Adopting a structured and strategic approach, combined with an understanding of the tools and practices at disposal, can substantially enhance the efficiency and effectiveness of debugging efforts in Smalltalk programming.

6.11 Logging and Monitoring in Smalltalk Applications

Logging and monitoring are indispensable techniques for diagnosing issues, understanding application behavior, and improving performance. In Smalltalk, these practices can be integrated into applications to facilitate the identification of errors, track application metrics, and monitor runtime operations.

Implementing Logging in Smalltalk

To implement logging in Smalltalk applications, developers can utilize the Transcript tool or create custom logging mechanisms. The Transcript is a global object used for printing messages to a console, suitable for simple logging requirements.

```
Transcript show: 'An error has occurred: ', errorMessage.
Transcript cr.
```

However, for more sophisticated logging needs, developers may implement a custom logging class. This class can be designed to record logs in various formats, such as plain text or JSON, and write them to different destinations, like files or remote log management systems.

```
LoggingClass>>logMessage: aMessage
    "Logs a message to a predefined log file"
    | logStream |
    logStream := FileStream fileNamed: 'application.log' mode: 'append'.
    logStream
        nextPutAll: (TimeStamp now printString , ' - ' , aMessage);
        cr;
        close.
```

Monitoring Application Performance

Monitoring application performance is crucial for maintaining the efficiency and reliability of Smalltalk applications. Smalltalk's integrated development environment (IDE) provides tools for performance profiling, which allows developers to analyze the time complexity of methods and identify bottlenecks.

To use the profiling tools, one can employ the `MessageTally` class. This class can tally the number of messages sent during the execution of a block of code and measure execution time.

```
MessageTally spyOn: [MyApplication new run].
```

The output from `MessageTally` includes a detailed report of the time spent executing each method, which is invaluable for pinpointing performance issues.

```
- 23.5% {117ms} MyApplication>>run
  - 23.5% {117ms} MyApplication>>heavyComputationMethod
    - 10.5% {52ms} AnotherClass>>timeIntensiveMethod
```

Best Practices for Logging and Monitoring

To ensure effective logging and monitoring of Smalltalk applications, developers should adhere to several best practices:

- Prioritize what to log by distinguishing between informational messages and error messages.
- Use a consistent log format that includes timestamps, log levels, and descriptive messages.
- Regularly review and analyze log files to identify patterns that may indicate underlying issues.
- Leverage performance profiling tools during development and testing phases to optimize application performance.
- Implement log rotation and archiving strategies to manage log file sizes and preserve historical data.

Logging and monitoring play a pivotal role in the development and maintenance of Smalltalk applications. By employing tools like the Transcript and leveraging classes like `MessageTally`, developers can effectively diagnose and resolve issues, enhance application performance, and ensure the reliability of their software solutions.

6.12 Common Errors and How to Troubleshoot Them

In the development of Smalltalk applications, certain errors are encountered more frequently than others. Recognizing these common errors and understanding how to troubleshoot them can significantly streamline the debugging process. This section delineates various typical errors, elucidates their causes, and proposes methodologies for resolving them efficiently.

Message Not Understood

One of the most prevalent errors in Smalltalk programming is the `MessageNotUnderstood` error. This error occurs when an object receives a message (method call) that it does not recognize. Typically, this is a result of either a misspelled method name or attempting to invoke a method not supported by the object's class.

To troubleshoot this error, ensure that:

- The method name is spelled correctly in the message send.
- The object is indeed an instance of the class you expect it to be. Sometimes, due to incorrect initialization or assignment, the object might not be of the expected class.

Here is an example that raises a `MessageNotUnderstood` error due to a typo in the method name:

```
aString := 'Hello, World!'.
aString revrse. % Incorrect method name
```

Nil References

Another common issue is attempting to send a message to a `nil` object. In Smalltalk, `nil` represents the absence of a value. Sending a message to `nil` will result in a `MessageNotUnderstood` error if the message is not explicitly handled by `nil`.

To prevent `nil` reference errors:

- Always initialize variables.
- Perform null checks before sending messages to objects that might be `nil`.

Dangling References

A "dangling reference" occurs when an object that has been released from memory is still being referenced elsewhere in the code. While Smalltalk's garbage collection handles memory management, dangling references can still lead to unexpected behavior or crashes if an object is manually released or becomes unreferenced due to scope termination.

To manage dangling references, it is advisable to:

- Avoid manual memory management wherever possible, relying instead on Smalltalk's garbage collection.
- Clear references to objects that are no longer needed by setting them to `nil`.

Debugging Tips

When troubleshooting the aforementioned errors or any other issue, the integrated development environment (IDE) provides essential tools for debugging. Using breakpoints, inspecting variables, and stepping through code execution are powerful techniques to isolate and resolve errors. Additionally, leveraging logging and monitoring can preemptively identify potential errors by tracking application behavior and state.

In summary, mastering the common errors in Smalltalk programming and their troubleshooting methods is a pivotal skill for developers. By adhering to best practices for error checking and utilizing the debugging tools available in the Smalltalk IDE, programmers can efficiently resolve issues and enhance the reliability of their Smalltalk applications.

Chapter 7

Graphical User Interface Programming with Morphic

Morphic is Smalltalk's powerful framework for creating and managing graphical user interfaces (GUIs), providing a dynamic and flexible environment for building interactive applications. This chapter introduces the fundamentals of GUI programming in Smalltalk using Morphic, including the creation of windows, dialogs, buttons, and handling user events. It delves into the concepts of layouts for designing responsive interfaces, customizing appearance, and integrating multimedia elements. Through practical examples and discussions on best practices, readers will learn to design and implement visually appealing and user-friendly interfaces in their Smalltalk applications.

7.1 Introduction to Morphic in Smalltalk

Morphic is an integral part of Smalltalk, offering an innovative and interactive framework for Graphical User Interface (GUI) programming. It allows developers to construct applications that are not only visually appealing but also highly interactive and responsive. Morphic stands out by enabling GUI components, known as "Morphs", to be composed in an agile and dynamic fashion. This trait makes Morphic particularly suitable for rapid application development and prototyping.

The core philosophy behind Morphic is direct manipulation. In a Morphic environment, every GUI element is an object that users can interact with directly. This approach contrasts with traditional event-driven GUI frameworks, where the flow of control is dictated by predefined user actions triggering events. Morphic's design emphasizes fluidity and immediacy, fostering a closer connection between the user interface and the application logic.

To start engaging with Morphic, one must first grasp its object-oriented nature. At its heart, Morphic is built around the concept of Morphs - the fundamental building blocks of any Morphic-based GUI. Each Morph is a living object in the Smalltalk environment, capable of displaying itself, handling user input, and interacting with other Morphs. This architecture not only simplifies GUI development but also encourages the exploration of creative and novel interaction paradigms.

```
"Creating a simple Morph"
| blueMorph |
blueMorph := Morph new.
blueMorph color: Color blue.
blueMorph extent: 100@100.
blueMorph openInWorld.
```

The above code snippet demonstrates the creation of a basic Morph. Here, a new instance of `Morph` is created, assigned a color, given dimensions (extent), and finally, displayed in the World, Morphic's top-level canvas. This example encapsulates the simplicity and expressiveness inherent in Morphic programming.

In terms of user input handling, Morphic provides an event dispatch mechanism that supports a wide range of interactions, from mouse clicks to keyboard entries. Morphs can override default event handling methods to implement custom behavior, thus offering extensive flexibility in UI design.

$$\text{Let } e \text{ denote an event.} \tag{7.1}$$
$$\text{Define } handleEvent(e) \text{ as a custom event handling method.} \tag{7.2}$$

The mathematical notation emphasizes the transformative nature of handling events in a Morphic ecosystem. Here, $handleEvent(e)$ symbolizes a method that takes an event e and processes it, potentially altering the state of a Morph or triggering application-specific logic.

Morphic's architecture is inherently hierarchical, wherein Morphs can contain other Morphs. This compositionality is pivotal for constructing complex interfaces, facilitating a modular and scalable approach to GUI development. For example, a window in Morphic may comprise multiple button Morphs, each of which could contain icon Morphs or text Morphs.

- Morphs are the basic building blocks in a Morphic interface.
- Every Morph is direct-manipulable and responsive to user interaction.
- Morphs can be composed to form complex and interactive GUIs.
- Custom behavior and appearance are achieved through overriding methods and properties.

Embracing Morphic in Smalltalk requires adopting a mindset where direct manipulation, object-orientation, and composability take precedence. Morphic's design not only caters to the construction of conventional GUI elements but also opens up possibilities for innovative user interactions and creative expression in interface design. As developers familiarize themselves with Morphic, they will uncover its potential to create applications that deeply engage and enthrall users.

7.2 Understanding Morphic's Architecture and Components

Morphic, as an innovative framework for GUI programming in Smalltalk, adopts a unique architecture that facilitates dynamic interactions within applications. At its core, Morphic is built around the concept of "morphs" – objects that represent both the visual and behavioral aspects of GUI components. This section will cover the hierarchical structure of Morphic, the role of the World and Hand in event handling, and the significance of Morphs and their subclasses.

The Hierarchical Structure

Morphic's design is inherently hierarchical, with the *World* morph at the top of this hierarchy. The World is essentially the canvas on which all other morphs are displayed. It acts as the root container that manages the layout and rendering of various GUI components. Below the World, we find a diverse range of morphs that can be complex (containing other morphs) or simple (standalone elements). This structure allows for a modular and flexible approach to GUI design, where components can be easily added, removed, or modified.

The Role of the World and Hand

The concept of the World is pivotal in managing the overall GUI environment. However, interaction within this environment is mediated by another critical component known as the *Hand*. The Hand represents the user's point of interaction, akin to a cursor, but with more sophisticated handling capabilities. It can pick up, move, and interact with morphs, facilitating direct manipulation of GUI elements by the user.

Understanding Morphs and Their Subclasses

At the heart of Morphic's architecture are morphs themselves. A morph can be understood as an encapsulation of both graphics (how it looks) and behavior (how it acts). Every morph in the hierarchy inherits from the `Morph` class, which provides basic functionalities such as rendering, event handling, and geometry management.

- **Basic Morphs:** These include simple shapes like rectangles, circles, and text fields. They serve as the building blocks for more complex interfaces.
- **Composite Morphs:** Composite morphs are aggregates of other morphs. They can be used to create complex GUI elements like toolbars, menus, and dialog windows.
- **Custom Morphs:** Developers can create custom morphs by subclassing the `Morph` class. This allows for the creation of unique GUI components tailored to specific application needs.

Customization and extension of morphs are facilitated through subclassing. For instance, creating a custom button involves subclassing a morph and overriding its event handling methods to respond to mouse clicks.

Event Handling in Morphic

Event handling is a critical aspect of GUI programming, and Morphic provides a robust mechanism for this. Events in Morphic are propagated through the morph hierarchy, starting from the morph under the Hand and then up through its ancestors. This allows for both specific and general event handling strategies.

```
"Example of event handling in a custom morph subclass"
MyCustomMorph >> handleMouseDown: anEvent
    super handleMouseDown: anEvent.
    "Custom behavior here"
```

In this example, `handleMouseDown:` is overridden to provide custom behavior when the user clicks on the morph. It calls the superclass method to ensure that any necessary default behaviors are executed before executing the custom code.

Understanding the architecture and components of Morphic is integral for effective GUI development in Smalltalk. The hierarchical nature, coupled with the flexibility offered by morphs and their subclasses, provides a powerful toolkit for creating interactive and responsive applications. Event handling mechanisms further enrich the interactive capabilities, enabling developers to capture and respond to user actions in a precise manner. As we progress, leveraging these concepts will be pivotal in designing and implementing sophisticated GUI elements.

7.3 Creating Basic Morphs: Windows, Dialogs, and Buttons

Creating basic morphs in Smalltalk using the Morphic framework involves the instantiation and manipulation of graphical objects such as windows, dialogs, and buttons. These elements serve as the foundational building blocks for building graphical user interfaces (GUIs) in Smalltalk applications. This section we will discuss the creation and customization of these basic morphs, using code examples and explanations to guide you through the process.

Windows

In Morphic, a window is an instance of the `SystemWindow` class. It acts as a container for other morphs and provides functionalities such as resizing, moving, and closure. To create a simple window, you can follow these steps:

```
| window |
window := SystemWindow new.
window label: 'My First Window'.
window openInWorld.
```

This code snippet creates a new instance of the `SystemWindow` class, sets the window's title to "My First Window," and then opens it. The method `openInWorld` is responsible for displaying the window on the screen.

Dialogs

Dialogs are special types of windows used to interact with the user, typically for input or to display messages. Morphic provides various dialog classes for different purposes, such as information dialogs, confirmation dialogs, and input dialogs. Here is an example of creating a simple information dialog:

```
UIManager default inform: 'Hello, Morphic!'.
```

This code uses the `UIManager` class to display an information dialog with the message "Hello, Morphic!". The `inform:` method is a convenient way to show quick messages to the user.

Buttons

Buttons are interactive morphs that users can click to perform actions. Creating a button involves creating an instance of the `SimpleButtonMorph` class and setting its properties, such as label and action. Below is an example of how to create a button that prints a message to the Transcript when clicked:

```
| button |
button := SimpleButtonMorph new.
button label: 'Click Me'.
button color: Color green.
button on: #click send: #value to: [Transcript show: 'Button was clicked'; cr].
button openInWorld.
```

In this example, a new button is created with the label "Click Me" and a green background color. The `on:send:to:` method is used to specify that when the button is clicked (`#click`), it should send the `#value` message to the given block of code, which prints "Button was clicked" to the Transcript. Finally, the button is displayed using `openInWorld`.

Creating basic morphs is the first step towards building complex and interactive GUIs in Smalltalk applications using the Morphic framework. By understanding how to instantiate and configure windows, dialogs, and buttons, developers can begin to construct user interfaces that facilitate user interaction and enhance the functionality of their applications.

7.4 Event Handling in Morphic: Responding to User Actions

In Smalltalk, Morphic is the engine that drives the graphical user interfaces (GUIs), making it possible to create highly interactive and responsive applications. A critical aspect of any GUI is its ability to handle user events, such as clicks, keyboard presses, and mouse movements. In this section, we will discuss the fundamentals of event handling within the Morphic framework, focusing on the mechanisms Smalltalk provides for detecting and responding to these user actions.

Morphic translates various user actions into events. Each event is an instance of an Event class or one of its subclasses. When a user interacts with a morph, for example, by clicking a button, Morphic generates an event object encapsulating the details of this interaction, such as the type of event (e.g., mouse click), the location of the cursor, and the morph that was interacted with.

To begin handling an event, a morph must first express its interest in certain types of events. This is achieved by overriding the morph's `handlesMouseDown:` method for mouse clicks, `handlesMouseUp:` for mouse release events, and `handlesMouseMove:` for mouse movement events, amongst others. Each of these methods returns a boolean value indicating whether the morph is interested in the specified type of event. For example, to make a morph responsive to mouse down events, you would override `handlesMouseDown:` to return `true`.

```
MyMorph>>handlesMouseDown: anEvent
  ^true
```

Once a morph has declared interest in an event, it must define how it responds to such events. This is done by implementing the appropriate event-handler method in the morph class. For instance, to react to a mouse click, the morph would provide an implementation for the `mouseDown:` method, which gets triggered by Morphic when a mouse down event occurs for that morph.

```
MyMorph>>mouseDown: anEvent
  "Implement the reaction to the mouse down event here"
```

Other event-handler methods include `mouseUp:` for mouse release events, `mouseMove:` for mouse movement events, `keyDown:` for key press events, and `keyUp:` for key release events. Each method receives an event object as its argument, from which information about the event can be extracted, such as the cursor's position for mouse events or the pressed key for keyboard events.

Event handling in Morphic also supports more complex interactions by allowing morphs to capture and retain the focus for events. This is particularly useful for drag-and-drop functionality, where a morph must continue to receive mouse movement events even if the cursor moves outside its boundaries. To facilitate this, Morphic provides methods like `morphToTakeFocus:`, which allows a morph to request event focus, and `releaseFocus`, for releasing it.

For illustrative purposes, consider implementing drag-and-drop functionality. The morph would capture focus on a mouse down event and release it on a mouse up event, updating its position according to the movement of the cursor.

```
MyMorph>>mouseDown: anEvent
  self morphToTakeFocus: anEvent.
```

```
MyMorph>>mouseMove: anEvent
```

```
  self position: (self position + anEvent delta).
```

```
MyMorph>>mouseUp: anEvent
  self releaseFocus.
```

Handling events in Morphic facilitates the creation of interactive and responsive morphs. Through the examples provided, it is evident that Smalltalk and the Morphic framework provide a robust and flexible toolset for capturing and responding to user actions, enabling developers to design engaging GUIs tailored to the requirements of their applications.

7.5 Using Layouts for Responsive GUI Design

Creating a responsive GUI design in Morphic necessitates an understanding of layouts and their role in adapting the interface to various screen sizes and orientations. The flexibility of Morphic's layout management enables developers to create interfaces that respond to resizing and reorientation, ensuring a consistent user experience across different devices.

Principles of Responsive Design in Morphic

Responsive GUI design in Morphic is built on the principle of dynamic resizing and repositioning of UI components, known as morphs, according to the available screen real estate. This requires the use of layout managers, which automatically adjust the size, position, and spacing of morphs within a container morph based on specified rules.

- **Proportional Layouts**: Components resize proportionally to the parent container, ensuring that they occupy a consistent percentage of the space.

- **Fixed Margins**: Maintaining consistent margins around components, regardless of the container size, to ensure a uniform appearance.

- **Automatic Wrapping**: Components automatically move to the next line or column if there is insufficient space, similar to text flow in a paragraph.

Implementing Layout Managers

Morphic provides various layout managers to facilitate responsive design. To implement a layout manager, one needs to create a container morph and assign it a specific layout manager. The following example demonstrates creating a horizontal layout that automatically adjusts the spacing and alignment of child morphs.

```
| container button1 button2 |
container := Morph new.
container layoutPolicy: RowLayout new.
container hResizing: #spaceFill; vResizing: #spaceFill.

button1 := Morph new.
button1 color: Color red.
container addMorph: button1.

button2 := Morph new.
button2 color: Color blue.
container addMorph: button2.

container openInWorld.
```

Here, a container morph is created, and its layout policy is set to `RowLayout`, which arranges child morphs in a horizontal row. The `hResizing` and `vResizing` properties of the container are set to `#spaceFill`, indicating that the container morph should expand to fill its parent morph. Two child morphs, `button1` and `button2`, are created, colored, and added to the container. When displayed, the layout manager ensures that the buttons are evenly spaced and aligned horizontally within the container.

Advantages of Using Layouts

The adoption of layout managers in Morphic presents several advantages:

- **Simplified GUI Adjustments**: By abstracting the details of component positioning and resizing, layout managers simplify the process of adapting the GUI to different screen sizes.
- **Enhanced User Experience**: Responsive designs ensure that the application remains usable and aesthetically pleasing across a wide range of devices and screen orientations.
- **Easier Maintenance**: Adjustments to the GUI, such as adding or removing components, become easier since the layout manager automatically handles the reorganization of the interface.

Leveraging Morphic's layout capabilities is crucial for developing responsive Smalltalk applications. By understanding and utilizing layout managers, developers can create interfaces that are both flexible and user-friendly, ensuring a consistent and appealing user experience regardless of the device or screen size.

7.6 Customizing Look and Feel with Morphic

Customizing the look and feel of graphical user interfaces (GUIs) in Morphic extends beyond mere aesthetic appeal; it significantly enhances user engagement and intuitiveness. Morphic, with its highly flexible architecture, permits an extensive range of customization options including colors, fonts, shapes, and even the behavior of GUI components. This section elucidates the methodologies for refining the visual and functional characteristics of Morphic-based interfaces.

To commence, let's tackle the customization of colors and fonts in Morphic. These elements play pivotal roles in ensuring readability and setting the tone of the user interface. In Morphic, each user interface component, or Morph, has properties that can be adjusted to modify its appearance. The following code snippet demonstrates how to adjust the background color and font of a button.

```
| button |
button := SimpleButtonMorph new.
button color: Color red.
button font: (TextStyle default fontOfSize: 18).
button label: 'Click Me'.
```

In this example, the `color:` method is employed to set the button's background color to red, while the `font:` method is used to specify the button's font size to 18. It's noteworthy that Morphic allows for a broad spectrum of colors supported by the Color class, providing the flexibility to enhance the user interface's visual appeal.

Moreover, customizing the shape of Morphs unlocks even more possibilities for interface personalization. Morphic offers a set of primitives to draw custom shapes, including rectangles, circles, and polygons. The code below illustrates how to create a custom-shaped Morph resembling an ellipse.

```
| customShape |
customShape := EllipseMorph new.
customShape color: Color blue.
customShape extent: 100@50.
customShape openInWorld.
```

Here, an instance of `EllipseMorph` is created and colored blue. The `extent:` method is utilized to define the ellipse's width and height, thereby illustrating the simplicity of crafting custom-shaped Morphs.

Addressing the requirement for responsive GUIs, Morphic provides layouts, such as flow, grid, and proportional layouts, to automatically adjust the positioning and sizing of components relative to the container Morph. Utilizing layouts is crucial for developing adaptable interfaces that perform seamlessly across diverse devices and screen sizes.

```
| container button1 button2 flowLayout |
container := Morph new.
button1 := SimpleButtonMorph new label: 'Button 1'.
button2 := SimpleButtonMorph new label: 'Button 2'.

```

```
flowLayout := FlowLayout new.
container layoutPolicy: flowLayout.

container addMorph: button1.
container addMorph: button2.
container openInWorld.
```

In this instance, `FlowLayout` is adopted to arrange two buttons horizontally within a container Morph. The `layoutPolicy:` method assigns the layout to the container, facilitating the automatic adjustment of its child Morphs according to the specified layout constraints.

Ultimately, incorporating multimedia elements such as images, sounds, and videos greatly enriches the UI experience. Morphic's architecture seamlessly supports multimedia integration, enabling the development of highly interactive and engaging applications. The subsequent code snippet highlights the inclusion of an image in a Morph.

```
| imageMorph image |
image := ImageMorph fromFileNamed: 'example.png'.
imageMorph := ImageMorph new image: image.
imageMorph openInWorld.
```

This example demonstrates the instantiation of an `ImageMorph` with an image retrieved from the file system. The `fromFileNamed:` method facilitates the loading of the image, which is then set to the `ImageMorph` instance, showcasing the simplicity of embedding multimedia content in Morphic-based interfaces.

In summation, Morphic's comprehensive suite of customization features empowers developers to create highly tailored, visually compelling, and functionally rich graphical user interfaces. Through the judicious application of colors, fonts, shapes, layouts, and multimedia elements, one can significantly augment the aesthetics and usability of Smalltalk applications, ensuring an optimal user experience.

7.7 Drawing and Graphics: Working with Canvas and Shapes

Morphic in Smalltalk provides a powerful canvas for drawing and handling shapes, enabling developers to enrich their applications with graphical elements. This section explores the use of Morphic's canvas for drawing operations and the manipulation of shapes, detailing the procedures required to create and manage complex graphical content.

Accessing the Morphic Canvas

To initiate drawing, one must first understand how to access the Morphic canvas. The canvas acts as a drawing surface on which shapes, lines, and text can be rendered. Here is a simple example that demonstrates how to access a canvas and prepare it for drawing:

```
| world aMorph canvas |
world := MorphicProject current world.
aMorph := Morph new.
world addMorph: aMorph.
canvas := aMorph canvas.
```

This code snippet creates a new Morph, adds it to the current world (the top-level container for all Morphs in a Morphic application), and retrieves the canvas of the newly added Morph. With the canvas obtained, one can proceed to perform various drawing operations.

Drawing Shapes

The canvas provides multiple methods for drawing basic shapes, including rectangles, ellipses, and polygons. The following code illustrates how to draw a rectangle and an ellipse on the canvas:

```
| rectangleBounds ellipseBounds |
rectangleBounds := 10@10 corner: 100@100.
ellipseBounds := 120@10 corner: 210@100.
canvas frameAndFillRectangle: rectangleBounds color: Color red.
canvas frameAndFillOval: ellipseBounds color: Color green.
```

The `rectangleBounds` and `ellipseBounds` variables define the coordinates and dimensions of the shapes to be drawn. The `@` operator is used to create points in Smalltalk. `frameAndFillRectangle:color:` and `frameAndFillOval:color:` methods draw a rectangle and an ellipse, respectively, filled with the specified color.

Working with Paths

For more complex shapes and drawings, one can use paths. A path is a sequence of lines and curves that can be combined to form intricate designs. The following example demonstrates how to create a simple path:

```
| path |
path := Path new.
path moveTo: (0@0).
path lineTo: (100@0).
path curveTo: (100@100) control1: (50@50) control2: (150@50).
canvas drawPath: path color: Color blue.
```

Here, a new path is created, starting at the point (0,0). A line is drawn to (100,0), followed by a curve to (100,100) with two control points specifying the curve's shape. Finally, the path is drawn on the canvas with a specified color.

Manipulating Graphics Context

The graphics context of a canvas provides numerous options to customize the appearance of drawings, such as setting the stroke width, the line pattern, and the fill pattern. Consider the following example, where various properties of the graphics context are adjusted:

```
canvas graphicsContext
    linePattern: (Array with: 5 with: 3);
    strokeWidth: 2.
canvas drawPath: path color: Color blue.
```

The `linePattern:` method sets the pattern of the lines to be drawn, in this case, a dash pattern represented by an array of lengths for the dashes and gaps. The `strokeWidth:` method adjusts the width of the lines.

Drawing and graphics in Smalltalk using Morphic provides a rich set of features for creating dynamic and visually appealing applications. Through understanding and utilizing the canvas, along with Morphic's drawing primitives and manipulations, developers can efficiently incorporate graphical elements into their Morphic applications, enhancing both the user interface and the user experience.

7.8 Integrating Multimedia: Images, Sound, and Video

Integrating multimedia elements such as images, sound, and video into Morphic applications enhances the immersive experience for users. This section will cover the procedures to embed these types of content into a graphical user interface (GUI) using Smalltalk's Morphic framework.

Integrating Images

To incorporate images into Morphic, the `ImageMorph` class is utilized. The following steps delineate the process of displaying an image:

- Load the image file into the Smalltalk environment. This can be achieved with the `Form` class, which represents bitmapped images.
- Create an instance of `ImageMorph` and assign the loaded image as its contents.
- Add the `ImageMorph` instance to a parent morph, such as a window or panel, to display it in the GUI.

```
| image form imageMorph |
image := 'path/to/image/file.png'.
form := Form fromFileNamed: image.
```

```
imageMorph := ImageMorph new.
imageMorph image: form.
self addMorph: imageMorph.
```

Playing Sound

For audio playback in Morphic applications, the `SampledSound` class is utilized for handling sound files. The key steps for integrating and playing sound are as follows:

- Load the sound file. This is performed by creating an instance of the `SampledSound` class, which can load WAV files from the file system.
- Use the `play` method to start audio playback.

```
| sound |
sound := SampledSound fromFileNamed: 'path/to/sound/file.wav'.
sound play.
```

Embedding Video

Embedding video within a Morphic interface requires more sophisticated handling. While Morphic does not provide built-in support for video playback, integration can be achieved through external libraries or plugins specifically designed for media playback within Smalltalk environments. The process typically involves:

- Utilizing an external library compatible with Smalltalk for video playback.
- Creating a wrapper or interface within the Morphic framework to control and display the video content.
- Handling user interactions, such as play, pause, and stop commands, through Morphic's event-handling mechanisms.

Given the complexity and variability of video integration, developers are encouraged to refer to specific documentation of the library or plugin chosen for video playback functionality.

Integrating multimedia into Morphic applications significantly enriches the user interface, making applications more engaging and versatile. By following the outlined steps and utilizing Smalltalk's capabilities, developers can embed images, sound, and video into their Morphic-based applications, enhancing both aesthetics and functionality.

7.9 Building Interactive Applications with Morphic

Building interactive applications with Morphic entails several nuanced steps, each designed to harness the framework's dynamic capabilities for creating responsive and engaging GUIs. This section will guide through the creation of a simple drawing application, which exemplifies the integration of various Morphic components and events to produce a cohesive and interactively rich user experience.

First, let's instantiate a main window for our application. Morphic windows are created by instantiating the `SystemWindow` class, setting its title, and specifying dimensions that dictate its initial appearance on the screen.

```
| window |
window := SystemWindow new.
window label: 'Simple Drawing App'.
window extent: 300@200.
```

The `@` symbol is used to combine numbers into a point that specifies size or location dimensions, where the first number represents the width and the second number the height.

Next, we introduce a drawing canvas into our application window. The canvas is where users will perform drawing actions. Morphic's `SketchMorph` class is suited for this purpose. It offers a blank area that can track and respond to mouse events, making it ideal for drawing operations.

```
| canvas |
canvas := SketchMorph new.
window addMorph: canvas frame: (0@0 corner: 1@1).
```

Note that the frame of the canvas is set relative to the window's dimensions, allowing the canvas to automatically adjust its size with window resizing, leveraging Morphic's layout management capabilities.

Interaction with the canvas requires event handling for mouse actions. Typically, drawing applications respond to mouse down, move, and up events to draw lines or shapes. Here's how to add a simple event handler to our `SketchMorph` for drawing points on the canvas.

```
canvas on: #mouseDown send: #drawPoint: to: canvas.
canvas on: #mouseMove send: #drawPoint: to: canvas
    when: [:event | event hand buttonState = 2].
```

The `drawPoint:` method should be implemented in the `SketchMorph` class or an appropriate subclass to perform the actual drawing. It typically utilizes the `Canvas` class's drawing methods to render graphics based on user input.

The condition in `mouseMove` event handler ensures that drawing occurs only while the mouse button is pressed, using `buttonState = 2` to check the state of the mouse button.

To enrich the drawing experience, offering options for changing colors or brush sizes can be accomplished by integrating additional UI components like buttons or sliders. These components respond to user selections, adjusting the drawing behavior accordingly.

```
| colorPicker brushSizeSlider |
colorPicker := UIPainter new openAsMorph.
brushSizeSlider := SliderMorph new.
window addMorph: colorPicker frame: (0.0@0.0 corner: 0.2@0.1).
window addMorph: brushSizeSlider frame: (0.0@0.1 corner: 0.2@0.2).
```

Methods for changing colors or brush sizes can be similarly linked to these components via event handlers, dynamically altering the drawing characteristics based on user inputs.

Finally, integrating multimedia elements like images or sounds in response to certain actions (for instance, playing a sound when a drawing action is completed) can further enhance the interactive experience. This would typically involve loading multimedia resources and triggering their playback or display under specific conditions.

Building interactive applications with Morphic, as illustrated in this simple drawing app example, showcases the framework's potential for creating rich, responsive GUIs. By leveraging Morphic's component integration and event handling capabilities, developers can implement a wide range of interactive features, enhancing the usability and engagement of their Smalltalk applications.

7.10 Advanced Topics: Morphic 3D and Animations

Morphic in Smalltalk provides a robust platform not only for creating two-dimensional graphical user interfaces but also for venturing into the realm of 3D graphics and animations. This section explores the extension of Morphic to support 3D graphics display and animations, critical for developing dynamic and interactive applications.

The journey into 3D graphics with Morphic begins with understanding the coordination between Morphic's existing 2D capabilities and the additional components required for 3D rendering. Morphic's architecture is designed around the concept of morphs - objects that represent visual elements on the screen. To incorporate 3D graphics, it is essential to introduce a new kind of morph, herein referred to as `3DMorph`, which serves as the bridge between Morphic's 2D environment and the 3D graphics engine.

Creating a `3DMorph` requires dealing with three-dimensional spaces, which means that every `3DMorph` has a position defined by three coordinates (x, y, and z), and can be rotated around the three axes. The following is an example code snippet that demonstrates how to create a simple 3DMorph:

```
3DMorph new
    position: (0@0@0);
    color: Color blue;
    extent: (100@100@100);
    yourself.
```

Managing 3D graphics also involves dealing with perspectives and camera positions since the view of a 3D scene changes based on the viewer's location relative to the scene. Morphic simplifies this by encapsulating camera controls within the 3D environment, allowing the developer to focus on designing the scene rather than the underlying complexities of 3D rendering.

Animating morphs in Morphic, whether 2D or 3D, is achieved through manipulating their properties over time. An animation sequence can be defined where properties such as position, color, and scale are changed in small increments in each frame of the animation. Here is an example of a simple animation loop that moves a morph across the screen:

```
(1 to: 100) do: [:i |
    myMorph position: (myMorph position + (1@0@0)).
    World doOneCycle.
    (Delay forMilliseconds: 20) wait.
].
```

This code snippet effectively moves `myMorph` horizontally across the screen, with a delay of 20 milliseconds between each incremental move, creating the illusion of motion.

When dealing with 3D animations, the principle remains the same, but one must consider the changes in the z-axis as well, and possibly the rotations around any of the three axes. Additionally, 3D animations can become computationally intensive, requiring optimization techniques such as culling, which involves not rendering objects that are not currently visible to the viewer, to maintain smooth performance.

```
Animation Frame 1: Morph at (10, 20, 30)
Animation Frame 2: Morph at (11, 21, 31)
Animation Frame N: Morph at (N+10, N+20, N+30)
```

Moreover, when incorporating animations and 3D graphics into applications, it is imperative to keep user interaction in mind. Morphic's event handling system, which was discussed in earlier sections, extends naturally to 3D morphs and animations, allowing developers to create interactive 3D applications where user actions can trigger animations or transformations in the 3D space.

Lastly, optimizing the performance of Morphic applications that utilize 3D graphics and animations involves careful management of resources. Developers should consider the implications of rendering complex 3D scenes and strive to balance visual fidelity with application responsiveness. Techniques such as level of detail (LOD) rendering, where the complexity of 3D models is adjusted based on their distance from the camera, can significantly enhance performance while preserving visual quality.

Extending Morphic's capabilities to include 3D graphics and animations opens up a vast array of possibilities for Smalltalk developers. By leveraging these advanced features, one can create not only visually appealing applications but also ones that are dynamic and interactive, thus enhancing the user experience. With careful planning and optimization, the challenges of working with 3D graphics and animations can be effectively managed, allowing developers to fully harness the power of Morphic in their applications.

7.11 Debugging and Optimizing Morphic Applications

Debugging and optimizing Morphic applications in Smalltalk involves a systematic approach to identify bottlenecks and errors, and implementing strategies to enhance performance and reliability. This section covers effective techniques and tools for debugging and optimizing Morphic-based GUI applications.

Profiling Morphic Applications

Profiling is the first step in optimizing any application. It allows developers to identify performance hotspots by analyzing the time complexity and memory usage of different parts of the application. In Smalltalk, the MessageTally class provides a simple way to profile applications.

```
MessageTally spyOn: [MyMorphicApplication new openInWorld].
```

The above code snippet launches the Morphic application and profiles its execution, providing a breakdown of method calls and their execution time. This information is crucial for pinpointing inefficiencies in the application.

Reducing Rendering Overheads

Rendering is a critical part of any GUI application and can significantly affect performance. In Morphic, minimizing the number of redraws and optimizing redraw regions can lead to substantial performance improvements.

- Use `Owner.corner:` sparingly as it triggers a complete redraw of the component and its subcomponents. Instead, opt for `invalidateLayout` or `invalidate` where appropriate.

- Leverage `deferUpdatesWhile:` for batch updates to the GUI to minimize redraws.

```
world deferUpdatesWhile: [
    world submorphsDo: [:each | each color: Color random].
].
```

- When dealing with custom morphs, override the `drawOn:` method efficiently to draw only the necessary parts.

Memory Management

Proper memory management is essential for maintaining the responsiveness and stability of Morphic applications. Smalltalk provides garbage collection, but developers still need to manage references to ensure that unused objects are collected.

- Regularly inspect and clean up global variables or caches holding onto morph instances that are no longer in use.
- Use `WeakArray` or `WeakDictionary` for caches or collections of morphs to allow them to be garbage collected when no longer referenced elsewhere.

Optimizing Event Handling

Event handling can become a source of bottlenecks, especially in complex applications with many interactive elements. Efficiently managing event listeners and handlers is key to maintaining smooth user interactions.

- Minimize the work done in event handlers; defer heavy computations to background processes if possible.
- Use `EventFilter` to pre-process or selectively pass events to handlers to avoid unnecessary computations.

Leveraging Caching

Caching is an effective technique for optimizing applications, particularly those involving expensive computations or resource loading (e.g., images or data from a database).

```
| cache key result |
cache := Dictionary new.
key := 'expensiveComputation'.

result := cache at: key ifAbsent: [
    "Perform expensive computation or resource loading"
```

```
    | computationResult |
    computationResult := self performExpensiveComputation.
    cache at: key put: computationResult.
    computationResult.
].
```

In the above example, a dictionary is used as a simple cache. Before performing an expensive computation, the cache is checked. If the result is already cached, it is returned immediately, avoiding the need for recomputation.

Through careful application of these debugging and optimization techniques, developers can significantly improve the performance and reliability of Morphic applications in Smalltalk, ensuring a smooth and responsive user experience.

7.12 Best Practices for GUI Development in Smalltalk

In ensuring effective Graphical User Interface (GUI) development in Smalltalk, adherence to a set of best practices is crucial. These guidelines have been distilled from extensive experience and knowledge acquisition within the realm of Smalltalk's Morphic framework. Morphic, a cornerstone in Smalltalk for GUI programming, demands a nuanced understanding and application of these practices to achieve optimal results in terms of functionality, reliability, and user experience.

The first best practice revolves around the modular design of Morphic components. Modularization enables the development of reusable and comprehensible code, which significantly reduces complexity in large GUI projects. For instance, if a developer is creating multiple interactive panels within an application, defining each panel as a separate Morph and then composing these Morphs into the final application pane enhances maintainability and modularity.

```
Morph newPanel := MyCustomPanel new.
newPanel position: (100@200).
```

```
world addMorph: newPanel.
```

```
Panel Added at Position: 100@200
```

Developers are encouraged to encapsulate functionalities within these modular components, using method clarity and conciseness as benchmarks for quality code.

Another key practice is the effective management of events. In Morphic, event handling is pivotal for creating interactive applications that respond aptly to user inputs. Implementing an efficient event delegation model ensures that events are processed and responded to in a timely and logical manner. The following code sample illustrates a basic event handling setup:

```
myButton on: #click do: [self performAction].
```

This example demonstrates the association of a click event with a button, employing a simple and direct approach to event handling widely recommended in Smalltalk development.

For designing responsive UIs, the utilization of layouts in Morphic is not just recommended but essential. Layouts manage the size and position of each component relative to the container Morph, allowing GUIs to adapt effortlessly to different screen sizes and resolutions. It is advisable to deeply understand and leverage the various layout options available in Morphic to achieve responsive design.

```
myPanel layoutPolicy: TableLayout new.
myPanel listDirection: #leftToRight.
myPanel hResizing: #spaceFill.
myPanel vResizing: #spaceFill.
```

This code snippet configures a panel to use a table layout that adjusts items from left to right, filling the available space both horizontally and vertically, a practice that significantly improves the adaptability of GUI components.

Customizing the look and feel of GUI components not only enhances aesthetics but also improves user engagement and satisfaction. Morphic's flexible styling options allow developers to adjust the visual appearance of Morphs extensively. Beyond the default settings, it is advisable to explore and implement custom themes and styles to ensure that the application stands out and aligns with brand identity or project requirements.

```
myButton color: Color red.
myButton borderWidth: 2.
myButton borderColor: Color black.
```

Proper documentation and comments within the GUI codebase cannot be overstated. Despite the graphical nature of the work, future maintainability and scalability significantly depend on the clarity of the code. Comprehensive comments and documentation facilitate easier onboarding for new developers and assist in debugging or expanding existing projects.

Regarding performance optimization, iterating over GUI components to identify and rectify performance bottlenecks is crucial. This may involve refining event handling mechanisms, optimizing layout computations, or limiting the redrawing of components to necessary instances only. Monitoring tools and profiling are valuable in this pursuit, enabling developers to pinpoint inefficiencies and apply targeted optimizations.

In summary, mastering GUI development in Smalltalk using the Morphic framework demands a commitment to best practices that span design, implementation, and optimization phases. By modularizing components, efficiently handling events, utilizing layouts for responsive design, customizing component appearances, diligently documenting code, and continuously seeking performance improvements, developers can craft superior and engaging GUI applications that stand the test of time in functionality and design.

Chapter 8

Developing Web Applications with Seaside

Seaside represents a revolutionary approach to web application development in Smalltalk, simplifying the complexities traditionally associated with web development. This chapter offers an in-depth exploration of developing web applications using Seaside, guiding readers through setting up a development environment, creating simple to complex web applications, and managing user input and session state. It also covers the integration of databases, adding dynamic content with AJAX, and the application of CSS for styling. Through comprehensive coverage of these topics, readers will acquire the skills necessary to create robust, scalable web applications leveraging Seaside's capabilities in the Smalltalk environment.

8.1 Introduction to Seaside: A Smalltalk Web Framework

Seaside marks a significant departure from traditional web development frameworks. By leveraging the power and simplicity of Smalltalk, Seaside provides an expressive platform for building web applications. Unlike other frameworks that follow the request-response paradigm rigidly, Seaside enables a more natural flow of control, akin to desktop application development. This is achieved through its innovative session management and component-based structure, allowing developers to manage complex interactions with ease.

Core Principles of Seaside

- **Component-Based Architecture:** In Seaside, applications are composed of reusable components. Each component is responsible for rendering a part of the web page and handling user interactions. This encapsulation facilitates the development of complex user interfaces in a modular and manageable way.
- **Continuation-Based Flow:** Seaside uses continuations to maintain application state across user requests. This allows developers to write web applications in a linear and stateful manner, despite the stateless nature of the HTTP protocol. This paradigm shift simplifies the handling of user interaction flows, such as multi-step forms or wizards.
- **Integrated Development Environment (IDE) Support:** Seaside seamlessly integrates with Smalltalk's development environment. This integration provides developers with powerful tools for code browsing, debugging, and testing Seaside applications directly within the IDE. The immediate feedback loop this creates accelerates development and enhances code quality.
- **Built-in Support for AJAX and JavaScript:** Seaside

incorporates support for AJAX, allowing developers to create highly interactive web applications. Coupling AJAX with Smalltalk's powerful language features enables the development of rich user experiences with minimal boilerplate JavaScript code.

Creating a web application in Seaside starts with defining components. Components are the building blocks of a Seaside application, encapsulating both the presentation and behavior of parts of your application. Each component in Seaside inherits from the class `WAComponent`, which provides the basic interface needed for rendering content and handling actions.

To illustrate, consider a simple counter component. This component renders a count on the webpage and provides buttons to increment or decrement the count.

```
WAComponent subclass: #Counter
    instanceVariableNames: 'count'
    classVariableNames: ''
    package: 'MyApp'

Counter>>initialize
    super initialize.
    count := 0.

Counter>>renderContentOn: html
    html heading: count.
    html form: [
        html submitButton
            callback: [count := count + 1];
            text: 'Increase'.
        html submitButton
            callback: [count := count - 1];
            text: 'Decrease'].
```

In the code above, the `Counter` class defines a simple Seaside component. The `initialize` method sets the initial count to 0. The `renderContentOn:` method uses the Seaside HTML builder API to render the current count and two buttons for increasing and decreasing the count. The callbacks attached to these buttons modify the `count` instance variable and trigger a re-render of the component.

This example demonstrates the elegance of Seaside's component model and its ability to encapsulate state and behavior within web components. The declarative nature of the component's user interface and interaction logic facilitates the development of both simple and complex web applications with rich user interfaces.

To conclude, Seaside stands out as a web framework by offering a set of features that embrace the dynamic capabilities of Smalltalk, making web development more natural and productive. Through its component-based architecture, continuation-based flow management, and seamless IDE integration, Seaside simplifies web application development and enables developers to build complex web applications with ease.

8.2 Setting Up Your Seaside Development Environment

To develop Seaside applications effectively, establishing a solid development environment is imperative. This section will explore the required software installations, including the Smalltalk IDE and the Seaside web framework. Moreover, we will outline the process of configuring these tools to work together seamlessly, preparing participants for subsequent development activities.

Installing the Smalltalk IDE

Seaside applications are developed within a Smalltalk integrated development environment (IDE). Pharo Smalltalk is the recommended IDE for its modern features and supportive community. Proceed with the following steps to install Pharo:

- Navigate to the Pharo download page using a web browser.
- Choose the version compatible with your operating system (Windows, macOS, Linux).
- Download the installer or archive file.

- Run the installer or extract the archive to a desired location on your system.

- Launch Pharo Launcher from the installed location to manage and create Pharo images.

After installation, Pharo Launcher provides a graphical interface to create, delete, and open Pharo images. Each image serves as an isolated Smalltalk environment for project development.

Installing Seaside into Pharo

With Pharo installed, the next step involves incorporating Seaside into your Pharo image. Seaside can be installed directly through the Pharo catalog. Execute the following steps within Pharo:

```
Iceberg enableMetacelloIntegration: true.
Metacello new
    baseline: 'Seaside3';
    repository: 'github://SeasideSt/Seaside:master/repository';
    load.
```

This code snippet utilizes Metacello—a package management system for Smalltalk—to fetch and install the latest version of Seaside from its GitHub repository.

Verifying the Installation

To confirm the successful installation of Seaside in your Pharo image, initiate a basic Seaside server and access it through a web browser:

```
(ZnServer startOn: 8080)
    delegate: (WAAdmin register: MyFirstComponent asApplicationAt: 'test').
```

Replace `MyFirstComponent` with any Seaside component you intend to use for this test. Navigate to `http://localhost:8080/test` in your web browser. If installation was successful, your Seaside component's rendered output should be displayed.

Configuring the Development Environment

Fine-tuning your development environment for Seaside involves a few additional steps:

- **Version Control:** Configure Iceberg for Git integration in Pharo to manage your Seaside projects. Iceberg seamlessly integrates with Pharo, providing an intuitive interface for version control operations.
- **Seaside Configuration Tools:** Familiarize yourself with Seaside's control panel for managing applications and server settings. Access the control panel by visiting `http://localhost:8080/config`.
- **Installing External Libraries:** Some Seaside applications may require JavaScript, CSS, or additional Smalltalk libraries. These can be installed using the Metacello and Iceberg tools, analogous to installing Seaside.

To expedite development, consider customizing the Pharo IDE with shortcuts and preferences suited to your workflow. Explore Pharo's settings and extensions to tailor the environment further.

Successfully setting up your Seaside development environment lays the foundation for building sophisticated web applications. This configuration not only facilitates the exploration of Seaside's capabilities but also integrates with broader web technologies, paving the way for comprehensive web development using Smalltalk.

8.3 First Steps: Creating a Simple Seaside Application

In this section, we will discuss the initial process required to create a simple web application using Seaside. The focus will be on establishing a foundational understanding of the essential steps: from registering your application within the Seaside framework to running it on a local server.

Registering the Application with Seaside

The first step in creating a Seaside application involves registering the newly created application with the Seaside framework. Registration allows Seaside to recognize the application and serve it through its integrated HTTP server.

The registration process can be accomplished with the following Smalltalk code snippet:

```
MySeasideApp registerAsApplication: 'my-first-seaside-app'
```

This line of code tells Seaside to register an instance of the MySeasideApp class as a web application accessible via the URL path 'my-first-seaside-app'.

Defining Components

Seaside applications are built using components. A component in Seaside represents a piece of the user interface, which can be as simple as a button or as complex as a form with multiple fields.

To define a component in Seaside, create a subclass of WAComponent. For example:

```
WAComponent subclass: #MyFirstComponent
    instanceVariableNames: ''
    classVariableNames: ''
    poolDictionaries: ''
    category: 'My-Seaside-Apps'
```

This code snippet creates a new component named MyFirstComponent, which is a direct subclass of WAComponent, Seaside's base component class.

Implementing Render Content

Every component in Seaside needs to implement a method to render its content on the web page. This is typically done by overriding the renderContentOn: method.

```
MyFirstComponent>>renderContentOn: html
    html heading: 'Welcome to Seaside'.
    html paragraph: 'This is your first component'.
```

In this example, the `renderContentOn:` method uses the HTML canvas to render a heading and a paragraph on the web page.

Running the Application

With the application registered and a component defined, the next step is to run the Seaside application. Seaside includes a built-in development server, making it straightforward to launch applications locally for testing and development purposes.

To start the server and access the application, follow these steps:

- Open the Seaside Control Panel within your Smalltalk environment.
- Start the Seaside HTTP server by selecting the appropriate option.
- Open a web browser and navigate to `http://localhost:8080/my-first-seaside-app`.

This will display the web page with the content rendered by the `MyFirstComponent` component.

By registering the application, defining a component, implementing the rendering logic, and running the local server, a basic Seaside web application is created. This simple application serves as a foundation, demonstrating the ease with which web applications can be developed using the Seaside framework. In subsequent sections, we will build upon this foundation, exploring more advanced features and concepts essential for developing robust web applications in Seaside.

8.4 Understanding Seaside Components and Their Lifecycle

Let's delve into the core concept of Seaside that distinguishes it from traditional web application frameworks: components and their lifecycle. Seaside employs a component-based architecture, which allows developers to construct web applications as a composition of reusable building blocks known as components. Each component in Seaside encapsulates both the logic and the presentation of a part of the web application, promoting modularity and reuse.

A component in Seaside is essentially a Smalltalk object that inherits from the `WAComponent` class. This inheritance confers upon the object the ability to participate in the Seaside application lifecycle, rendering HTML content, handling user inputs, and managing its state across HTTP requests.

The Lifecycle of a Seaside Component involves several key stages:

- **Initialization:** A component is instantiated by Seaside when incorporated into a web application. Here, developers have the opportunity to set up any necessary initial state in the component. This setup often involves initializing variables or configuring settings that influence the component's behavior.

```
myComponent := MyComponent new.
myComponent initialize.
```

- **Rendering:** During this phase, Seaside invokes the component to generate its corresponding HTML content. The component responds by executing its rendering logic, which typically involves invoking Seaside's HTML generation APIs.

```
renderContentOn: html
   html div
      class: 'my-component';
      with: 'Hello, Seaside!'.
```

- **Handling User Input:** If the rendered HTML includes form elements or interactive content, Seaside manages the HTTP requests triggered by user actions. It delegates to the component the task of processing these requests, allowing it to react to user inputs by updating its state or executing specific logic.

- **Updating and Redrawing:** In response to user actions or other events, a component may need to update its internal state and redraw its HTML content. Seaside ensures that the component's rendering method is called again, allowing the component to reflect the latest state in its output.
- **Cleanup:** Finally, when a component is no longer needed, Seaside provides an opportunity for the component to perform any necessary cleanup operations, such as releasing resources or removing event listeners.

Understanding Session Management and Callbacks:

In addition to the basic lifecycle, it's crucial to understand how Seaside manages user sessions and the use of callbacks for dynamic user interaction:

- **Session Management:** Seaside automatically creates sessions to track the state of interactions with individual users. Components can store state in the session object, allowing Seaside to preserve the context of user interactions across HTTP requests.
- **Callbacks:** Seaside introduces a powerful mechanism for handling user inputs through the use of callbacks. Developers define callbacks as Smalltalk blocks or methods, which are executed in response to specific user actions, such as clicking a button or submitting a form.

```
renderContentOn: html
    html form: [
        html submitButton
            callback: [ self handleButtonClick ];
            with: 'Click Me'.
    ].
```

By mastering the lifecycle of components and effectively utilizing session management and callbacks, developers can build complex, interactive web applications in Seaside. This component-based approach, coupled with Seaside's powerful features, enables the creation of highly modular, maintainable, and scalable web applications within the Smalltalk environment.

8.5 Using Seaside for Handling User Inputs and Forms

Handling user input is a fundamental aspect of developing interactive web applications. Seaside provides a simple yet powerful framework for managing forms and user inputs, enabling developers to create intuitive and responsive user experiences. This section will examine how to use Seaside to handle forms, manage input validation, and respond to user actions.

To start, let's create a basic form in Seaside. Forms in Seaside are defined within the `renderContentOn:` method of a component. The method `html form: []` is used to add a form to the webpage. Inside this block, input elements like text inputs, checkboxes, and buttons can be placed. Below is a simple example that creates a form with one text input field and a submit button.

```
renderContentOn: html
  html form: [
    html label: 'Enter your name'.
    html input
      callback: [:value | name := value];
      value: name.
    html submitButton
      callback: [self handleNameSubmission];
      with: 'Submit'.
  ].
```

In the above code, a form is created with a label, an input field, and a submit button. The `callback:` block associated with the input field is executed when the form is submitted. It receives the user's input as its argument, which can then be used within your application. Similarly, the submit button has a callback where you can define actions to take place after the form submission, such as processing the data or updating the user interface.

Validating user input is crucial for maintaining data integrity and providing feedback. Seaside allows you to easily add validation logic to your forms by utilizing callback blocks. If the input does not meet your criteria, you can render error messages and prevent the form from proceeding. Here is how you might implement simple input validation in Seaside:

```
handleNameSubmission
  | isValid |
  isValid := name size > 0.
  isValid ifFalse: [self inform: 'Name cannot be empty.'].
```

In this scenario, before proceeding with any form-related processing, the `handleNameSubmission` method checks whether the name entered by the user is not empty. If the validation fails, the user is informed with an appropriate message.

Seaside facilitates the handling of more complex forms and user interactions through its component-based architecture. Components can encapsulate parts of a form, enabling you to manage larger forms by dividing them into manageable pieces. This approach not only aids in organizing your application's UI logic but also promotes reuse of form elements across your application.

A significant advantage of using Seaside for form handling is its session management capabilities. User input can be seamlessly preserved across requests, simplifying the development of multi-page forms and complex user workflows. Seaside automatically takes care of the intricacies associated with maintaining session state, allowing you to focus on building your application's functionality.

```
renderContentOn: html
  html form: [
    html textInput
      on: #text of: self.
    html submitButton
      callback: [self processForm].
  ].
```

In this example, the `on:of:` method is used to bind the input field to a property of the component. This binding ensures that the input field's value is automatically updated within the component's state, simplifying data handling.

To conclude, Seaside provides an elegant and effective framework for handling user inputs and forms in web applications. Its straightforward API, combined with powerful session management and component-based architecture, empowers developers to create sophisticated and interactive web applications with ease.

8.6 Session Management in Seaside Applications

Session management is a critical component in web application development. It enables the application to preserve the state of interaction with an individual user across multiple requests. In Seaside, sessions are managed through the creation of session objects that encapsulate the state of a user session. This section will elucidate the mechanism of session management in Seaside, illustrating the instantiation, maintenance, and expiration of sessions, alongside practical examples for effective application.

Seaside provides a default session class named `WASession`. This class can be subclassed to store session-specific data and to implement session-related behavior. To begin with, let's instantiate a new session in Seaside:

```
MySession subclass: WASession [
    | userData |
]
```

In this code snippet, `MySession` is a subclass of `WASession`, capable of storing session-specific information in the variable `userData`. This subclassing approach enables developers to extend the base session functionality tailored to their specific application needs.

Each Seaside session is associated with a unique session key, typically managed through cookies or URL rewriting. The lifecycle of a session in Seaside begins when a user first accesses a Seaside application, and a new session object is created. This session persists across multiple requests by the same user until it either expires or is explicitly terminated.

Session expiration is a mechanism to eliminate outdated sessions and free resources. In Seaside, the expiration of a session is managed through the `WAApplication` class, which specifies the session timeout period. This period determines the duration of inactivity after which a session is considered obsolete and is automatically terminated. The default session timeout can be modified as follows:

```
WAApplication default expiryPolicy configuration at: #sessionTimeout put: 600.
```

This code snippet sets the session timeout to 600 seconds, after which inactive sessions will be expired and deleted.

To manage user-specific data within a session in Seaside, developers can utilize the session subclass created earlier. For instance, storing user input received from a form can be implemented as follows:

```
(MySession current userData) at: 'username' put: aUsername.
```

Here, `MySession current` retrieves the current session object, and user data is stored in the dictionary with the key 'username'.

Retrieving stored session data is equally straightforward:

```
| username |
username := (MySession current userData) at: 'username'.
```

This demonstrates how data associated with a user session can be stored and retrieved within a Seaside application, enabling personalized user interactions.

Effective management of sessions is crucial for maintaining a secure, consistent user experience in web applications. Seaside simplifies session management, offering mechanisms for session instantiation, maintenance, and expiration, which can be customized to suit the requirements of any application.

In the context of session management, security is paramount. Seaside sessions are inherently secure, with built-in mechanisms to prevent common security vulnerabilities such as session fixation and session hijacking. However, developers are advised to implement additional security measures, such as HTTPS and secure cookies, to guarantee the confidentiality and integrity of session data.

By mastering session management in Seaside, developers can create interactive, stateful web applications in Smalltalk, leveraging the distinctive features and flexibility of the Seaside framework to deliver a captivating user experience.

8.7 Integrating Seaside with Databases

Integrating Seaside with databases is a fundamental step in the development of full-fledged web applications. This process allows Seaside applications to persistently store, retrieve, and manipulate data, an essential requirement for most modern web applications.

To facilitate database integration, Seaside does not directly embed database access within its core framework. Instead, it relies on the flexibility and power of Smalltalk's ecosystem, which offers a variety of object-relational mapping (ORM) tools and database connectors. In this section, we will utilize GLORP (Generic Lightweight Object-Relational Persistence), one of the most widely used ORM libraries in the Smalltalk environment, to illustrate how to integrate a database into a Seaside application.

Setting up GLORP

Before integrating GLORP with Seaside, it is necessary to install the GLORP package in your Smalltalk environment. This process can vary depending on the specific Smalltalk distribution (e.g., Pharo, Squeak, VisualWorks) you are using. However, most environments allow package installation through their respective package managers or Monticello repositories.

Once GLORP is installed, you need to establish a connection to your database. GLORP supports multiple database systems, including but not limited to SQLite, PostgreSQL, and MySQL. For demonstration purposes, we will use SQLite due to its simplicity and ease of setup.

```
"Assuming you've already established a session"
dbSession := DatabaseAccessor forLogin: ((Login new)
    databaseClass: SQLiteDatabase;
    connectString: 'path/to/your/database.db';
    yourself).

"Register your session as the default"
DefaultDatabaseAccessor register: dbSession.
```

Defining Model Classes

With GLORP, you map your application's model classes to database tables. This mapping process instructs GLORP on how to translate between Smalltalk objects and database rows.

Consider a simple 'User' model with properties 'name' and 'email'. You will need to define this model class in your Smalltalk environment and then map it to a corresponding database table.

```
Object subclass: #User
    instanceVariableNames: 'id name email'
    classVariableNames: ''
    poolDictionaries: ''
    category: 'MyApplication-Models'.
```

The mapping for this 'User' class to a database table can be defined as follows:

```
descriptorForUser: aTable
    (aTable defineTable: 'users')
        defineColumn: 'id' type: platform serial.
    (aTable fieldNamed: 'id') bePrimaryKey.

    aTable defineColumn: 'name' type: (platform varChar: 255).
    aTable defineColumn: 'email' type: (platform varChar: 255).

    aTable createAccessor.
```

Performing CRUD Operations

With the models defined and mapped, you can now perform CRUD (Create, Read, Update, Delete) operations. GLORP allows you to execute these operations in an object-oriented fashion, abstracting away the raw SQL queries.

```
"Creating a new user"
user := User new.
user name: 'John Doe'.
user email: 'john.doe@example.com'.
dbSession inUnitOfWork: [dbSession registerAsNew: user].
dbSession commitUnitOfWork.

"Fetching a user by name"
users := dbSession read: User where: (Criteria field: #name) equals: 'John Doe'.

"Updating a user's email"
user email: 'new.email@example.com'.
dbSession inUnitOfWork: [dbSession registerAsDirty: user].
dbSession commitUnitOfWork.

"Deleting a user"
dbSession inUnitOfWork: [dbSession delete: user].
dbSession commitUnitOfWork.
```

Integrating a database into a Seaside application significantly enhances its capabilities, enabling the persistence and management of data. By leveraging Smalltalk's ORM libraries, such as GLORP, the integration process becomes streamlined, allowing developers to focus on the development of their application's core functionalities. This section provided a concise overview of setting up GLORP, defining model classes, mapping them to database tables, and performing CRUD operations. These operations form the foundation for developing dynamic, data-driven web applications with Seaside.

8.8 Adding AJAX and JavaScript to Your Seaside Apps

Seaside facilitates the incorporation of AJAX and JavaScript into Smalltalk web applications, enhancing interactivity and responsiveness without necessitating full page reloads for minor data updates or UI changes. Integrating AJAX into Seaside applications involves understanding the AJAX callback API provided by Seaside and employing JavaScript for client-side scripting.

To begin with AJAX in Seaside, one must first ensure that the JQuery library is loaded within the application. Seaside offers a seamless mechanism for this integration through the use of its resource management system. Including JQuery in a Seaside component can be achieved by overriding the `updateRoot:` method. Here is how it is typically done:

```
MySeasideComponent>>updateRoot: anHtmlRoot
    super updateRoot: anHtmlRoot.
    anHtmlRoot beHtml5.
    anHtmlRoot script: (anHtmlRoot javascript library: #JQuery).
```

With JQuery available, AJAX functionality can be implemented. For instance, consider a scenario where an application requires dynamically updating a part of the webpage based on user input, such as fetching and displaying data from the server without refreshing the page. This can be accomplished by using the AJAX callback API that Seaside provides.

Let's create a simple example where a button click in the UI triggers an AJAX call to the Seaside server, which then responds with a timestamp that gets displayed in the UI. The Seaside component setup could look something like this:

```
MySeasideComponent>>renderContentOn: html
    html div
        id: 'timestampContainer';
        with: 'Click the button to get the current time.'.
    html button
        onClick: (html jQuery ajax
                callback: [ :value | self updateTime ]
                script: [ :script |
                    script << (script jQuery: #timestampContainer)
                            html: [ :html | html render: self currentTime ] ]);
        with: 'Get Time'.
```

In the `renderContentOn:` method above, a `div` element with an ID of 'timestampContainer' is first rendered. This container will eventually display the timestamp received from the server. The `button`'s `onClick` event is then configured to make an asynchronous call to the server. The `callback:` block updates server-side state by calling `self updateTime`, while the `script:` block uses JQuery to update the HTML inside 'timestampContainer' with the new timestamp, through `self currentTime`.

The updateTime and currentTime methods, responsible for managing time on the server-side, are defined as:

```
MySeasideComponent>>updateTime
    currentTime := Time now.

MySeasideComponent>>currentTime
    ^ currentTime
```

Executing JavaScript directly to manipulate the DOM or to enhance the interaction experience can be done through Seaside's JS library integration. For a quick demonstration, let's say an application wants to display an alert dialog upon a certain server-side condition being met. This can be executed as follows:

```
(html javascript alert: 'This is an important message!') asFunction.
```

The snippet above defines an alert dialog to be displayed. It's encapsulated within a function to be executed whenever the specific condition occurs.

In addition to client-side functionality, AJAX in Seaside supports a broad spectrum of interactions, including but not limited to, form submissions, dynamic list updates, and real-time feedback systems. Combining AJAX and JavaScript extends the capabilities of Seaside applications significantly, providing a pathway to create highly interactive and user-friendly web applications.

By leveraging the AJAX and JavaScript support in Seaside, developers can enhance the user experience of their applications considerably. This entails not just updating the user interface asynchronously but also implementing complex client-side logic, animations, and interactions using JavaScript.

8.9 Styling Seaside Applications with CSS

Cascading Style Sheets (CSS) are vital for creating visually appealing web applications. Seaside offers several mechanisms to integrate CSS into your applications, ensuring both functionality and aesthetic appeal can be achieved seamlessly.

To incorporate CSS into a Seaside application, developers must understand how Seaside handles static and dynamic resources. Static resources are files, such as images or CSS files, that do not change often. Dynamic resources, on the other hand, may change content based on user interaction or other runtime conditions.

Incorporating Static CSS Files

For static CSS files, the most straightforward method is to place your CSS files within the web server's document root directory. Then, reference these CSS files in your Seaside components as needed.

```
html link
    rel: 'stylesheet';
    type: 'text/css';
    href: 'http://yourserver.com/css/yourStylesheet.css'.
```

This method directly inserts a link to the CSS file in the generated HTML, instructing the browser to apply these styles to the current page.

Embedding CSS Directly

Seaside also allows embedding CSS directly into components. This is particularly useful for small amounts of CSS or for styles specific to a component, which may not warrant a separate CSS file.

```
html style: 'body { font-family: sans-serif; }'
```

The above code snippet demonstrates how to embed CSS directly within a Seaside component. This method involves using the `style:` message to include CSS rules within the HTML header.

Using Seaside's CSS Builder

For a more dynamic approach, Seaside provides a CSS builder, enabling developers to generate CSS programmatically. This method offers flexibility in modifying styles based on runtime conditions.

```
WAComponent>>updateRoot: anHtmlRoot
    super updateRoot: anHtmlRoot.
    anHtmlRoot linkToStyle: (self class style).

WAComponent class>>style
    ^ WAStyleSheetBuilder new
        addRule: '#header' declarations: 'background-color: #EEE; color: #333;'
        addRule: 'h1' declarations: 'font-size: 2em;'
        yourself
```

In this example, the `updateRoot:` method is overridden in a Seaside component to include CSS generated by the `style` class method. The `style` method employs the `WAStyleSheetBuilder` to programmatically define CSS rules, which are then included in the page.

Strategies for Organizing CSS

Maintaining a structured approach to organizing CSS is crucial for scalability and maintainability. Consider separating styles into files based on their purpose (e.g., layout, typography, colors) and including them selectively in components that require them. It is beneficial to adopt naming conventions and comment extensively, particularly for large projects.

Through the methods outlined above, developers can effectively apply CSS to enhance the visual styling of their Seaside applications. Whether employing static CSS files, embedding styles directly, or using the CSS builder for dynamic generation, Seaside facilitates a flexible approach to styling, accommodating both the functional and aesthetic requirements of web application development.

8.10 Debugging and Testing Seaside Applications

Debugging and testing are crucial phases in the development lifecycle of any application, including web applications developed using Seaside in Smalltalk. These phases ensure the quality and reliability of the code before it reaches production environments. Seaside offers tools and practices adapted to its component-based architecture, facilitating a robust debugging and testing workflow.

Understanding Seaside Debugging Tools

Seaside integrates seamlessly with the Smalltalk environment, providing a rich set of debugging tools. One of the most powerful features is the built-in web-based debugger. Unlike traditional debugging tools, Seaside's debugger allows developers to interact with the live execution of an application directly through a web browser.

- **Web-based Debugger**: Activated upon encountering a runtime error, it allows developers to inspect the call stack, variables, and even modify the code on the fly. This immediate feedback loop significantly speeds up the debugging process in a Seaside application.
- **HALOs**: Seaside also offers HALOs, a set of dynamic tools that wrap around components. They provide quick access to debugging options, including viewing component structure, inspecting current state, and direct manipulation of properties.

To illustrate the use of the web-based debugger, consider the scenario where an unhandled exception is thrown during a user's interaction with the application. The Seaside web-based debugger can be invoked as follows:

```
"Simulating an error to trigger the debugger"
MySeasideComponent>>renderContentOn: html
    self error: 'Intentional Error for Demonstration'.
```

Upon executing this code during a session, the debugger window will open in the browser, showing detailed information about the error, including the stack trace.

Testing Strategies in Seaside

Testing in Seaside can take advantage of the comprehensive SUnit testing framework available in Smalltalk. SUnit is a unit testing framework that follows the xUnit testing methodology. Seaside extends this with specific testing tools that cater to web application testing needs.

- **SUnit Testing**: Basic unit tests in Seaside are written using the SUnit framework, testing individual components and functionality in isolation.
- **Seaside Testing Framework**: For more complex scenarios, such as testing interactions within a Seaside session or across components, Seaside provides a testing framework that simulates user interactions, such as clicking links or submitting forms.

An example of a simple SUnit test for a Seaside application component could be:

```
MyComponentTest>>testComponentRendersSomething
    | component html |
    component := MySeasideComponent new.
    html := component renderContentOn: (HTMLCanvas builder).
    self assert: html contents notEmpty.
```

This test instantiates a `MySeasideComponent` object and ensures that its `renderContentOn:` method produces non-empty HTML content.

Best Practices for Debugging and Testing

While the tools and strategies mentioned provide a solid foundation for debugging and testing Seaside applications, following best practices can further enhance the process:

- **Incremental Development**: Regularly test and debug during the development process to catch and resolve issues early.
- **Comprehensive Coverage**: Strive for wide test coverage, including unit, integration, and system tests, to ensure all aspects of the application are verified.

- **Test Simulated User Interactions**: Utilize Seaside's testing framework to simulate user interactions comprehensively, ensuring the UI behaves as expected.

Through the effective use of Seaside's debugging and testing tools, along with adherence to best practices, developers can significantly improve the reliability and quality of their web applications.

8.11 Deployment Strategies for Seaside Applications

Deploying Seaside applications involves several critical steps that ensure your web application is accessible, performant, and secure. This section will cover vital strategies including server selection, configuring deployment settings, the use of reverse proxies, and considerations for scaling and security.

Server Selection

The first step in deploying a Seaside application is selecting an appropriate server. The server must be compatible with Smalltalk and should support the Seaside framework. Pharo Smalltalk and GemStone/S are popular choices among developers for running Seaside applications. Each has its strengths, with Pharo being well-suited for rapid development and GemStone/S offering robust database solutions.

When choosing a server, consider the following factors:

- Compatibility with Seaside and the underlying Smalltalk version.
- Performance benchmarks for similar web applications.
- Support for SSL to enable HTTPS for secure connections.
- Server management tools and ease of deployment.

- Scalability options for future growth of the application.

Configuring Deployment Settings

Once a server has been selected, the next step is to configure the deployment settings specific to your Seaside application. This involves setting up the Seaside dispatcher and configuring session timeout values, logging, and error handling mechanisms. In a production environment, it is recommended to set the session timeout to a lower value to free server resources from inactive sessions.

For example, to set up a basic dispatcher in Seaside, use the following Smalltalk code snippet:

```
WAAdmin register: MyRootComponent asApplicationAt: 'myapp'.
```

This code registers `MyRootComponent` as the root component of the application accessible at the URL path '/myapp'.

Using Reverse Proxies

Using a reverse proxy, such as Nginx or Apache, in front of your Seaside application can greatly enhance its security and performance. The reverse proxy acts as an intermediary for requests from clients, forwarding them to the Seaside server. This setup allows for SSL termination, load balancing, and static content caching, which can significantly reduce the load on the Smalltalk server and improve response times.

To configure Nginx as a reverse proxy for a Seaside application, add the following to the Nginx configuration file:

```
location / {
    proxy_pass http://127.0.0.1:8080;
    proxy_set_header Host $host;
    proxy_set_header X-Real-IP $remote_addr;
    proxy_set_header X-Forwarded-For $proxy_add_x_forwarded_for;
}
```

This configuration directs all traffic to the Seaside application running on localhost port 8080, passing necessary headers for correct operation.

Scaling and Security

As your Seaside application grows in popularity, it may become necessary to scale your deployment to handle increased traffic. Techniques such as load balancing across multiple servers, session replication, and database clustering can help manage this growth. It is also crucial to prioritize security by regularly updating the server and Smalltalk environment, employing HTTPS, and safeguarding against common web vulnerabilities such as SQL injection and cross-site scripting (XSS).

In summary, deploying a Seaside application requires careful planning and consideration in server selection, deployment configurations, reverse proxy setup, and ongoing maintenance for scaling and security. By following these strategies, developers can ensure their Seaside applications are robust, secure, and capable of serving users efficiently.

8.12 Performance Tuning and Optimization in Seaside

Performance optimization in Seaside applications is critical for ensuring a smooth and responsive user experience. This section addresses various strategies and practices to diagnose and enhance the performance of Seaside web applications, focusing on both server-side and client-side optimizations.

Identifying Performance Bottlenecks

The first step in optimization is identifying the performance bottlenecks. Tools such as the Seaside Profiler can be instrumental in pinpointing areas of your application that are slow or inefficient. To activate the profiler in a Seaside application, one can integrate it into the application's configuration settings, allowing for the monitoring of request processing times and the identification of code that significantly impacts performance.

Server-Side Optimizations

Server-side optimizations primarily involve improving the response time and decreasing the resource consumption of your Seaside application.

- **Caching Content:** Implement caching strategies for frequently accessed content. Seaside supports caching at various levels, including component caching and HTTP caching. By storing rendered HTML of components or entire pages, the application can serve subsequent requests more rapidly.
- **Database Access and Indexing:** Optimize database interactions by ensuring efficient queries, proper indexing, and connection pooling. This reduces the latency in fetching data, significantly improving overall application performance.
- **Session Management:** Efficiently manage user sessions by limiting unnecessary session data storage and implementing session expiration policies to free up server resources.

Client-Side Optimizations

Client-side optimizations aim to enhance the application's responsiveness and reduce load times for the user. This includes minimizing the size and number of resources loaded by the browser.

- **Minimizing HTTP Requests:** Reduce the number and size of HTTP requests by combining CSS files, JavaScript files, and using sprites for images. This can be achieved manually or through tools that automate the process.

- **Using AJAX and JavaScript Efficiently:** Leverage AJAX to update only parts of a page rather than reloading the entire page. This reduces data transfer and improves user experience. However, ensure that AJAX calls are optimized and do not lead to excessive server requests.
- **CSS and JavaScript Minification:** Minify CSS and JavaScript files to reduce their size, thereby decreasing the time it takes for them to be downloaded and parsed by the browser.

Advanced Techniques

For applications with significant performance requirements, advanced optimization techniques may be necessary.

- **Load Balancing:** Deploying your Seaside application across multiple servers with load balancing can distribute the load, increasing the application's ability to handle high volumes of traffic.
- **Asynchronous Processing:** Utilize background processing for tasks that do not require immediate user interaction. This can improve the responsiveness of the application by performing long-running tasks asynchronously.

Performance tuning and optimization in Seaside applications is a multifaceted endeavor that involves both server-side and client-side strategies. By systematically identifying bottlenecks and applying targeted optimizations, developers can enhance the efficiency and user experience of their Seaside applications.

8.13 Exploring Advanced Seaside Features and Extensions

In this section, we will discuss the advanced features and extensions available in the Seaside web framework, which enable developers to build more complex and efficient web applications in Smalltalk. Seaside is known for its innovative approach to web development, making it easier to manage complexity and enhance the functionality of web applications without sacrificing performance or scalability.

To begin with, let's delve into the integration of jQuery and Scriptaculous libraries with Seaside. These JavaScript libraries offer a wide range of functionalities that can significantly enhance the user experience of web applications. Seaside provides seamless integration with these libraries, allowing developers to utilize advanced AJAX capabilities, animations, and user interface components with minimal effort.

```
html script: (html jQuery new draggable: #anElementId)
```

The above code snippet demonstrates how to make an HTML element draggable using jQuery in a Seaside application. Here, `#anElementId` represents the CSS ID of the HTML element you wish to make draggable. This is a simple example of how jQuery can be integrated into Seaside to add dynamic behavior to web pages.

Next, we explore the RESTful web services support in Seaside. REST (Representational State Transfer) is an architectural style that uses HTTP requests to communicate between clients and servers. Seaside provides facilities to develop RESTful applications, allowing developers to define URLs that respond to different HTTP methods such as GET, POST, PUT, and DELETE.

```
WAComponent subclass: #MyRestHandler
    instanceVariableNames: ''
    classVariableNames: ''
    poolDictionaries: ''
```

In the snippet above, a new subclass of `WAComponent` is defined, which can be used to handle RESTful requests. Seaside allows developers to map specific URLs to methods in these components, enabling the creation of RESTful web services that can be consumed by external clients.

Furthermore, Seaside's support for continuations is another powerful feature that facilitates complex flow control in web applications. Continuations allow developers to pause and resume computations at specific points, which can be incredibly useful for implementing multi-page workflows without losing the state.

```
self call: (MyComponent new)
```

The `call:` method is used to invoke another component from within a Seaside component, effectively pausing the current component and pushing the new component onto the call stack. The current state is preserved and can be resumed later, enabling complex navigational flows with minimal code.

Lastly, the Seaside testing framework, SUnit, provides a robust environment for testing Seaside applications. It allows developers to write unit tests for their components and run them in a simulated environment, ensuring the reliability and stability of the application.

```
TestCase subclass: #MyComponentTest
    instanceVariableNames: ''
    classVariableNames: ''
    poolDictionaries: ''

MyComponentTest >> testComponentBehavior
    self assert: (MyComponent new performAction) equals: expectedValue
```

In the example above, a subclass of `TestCase` is defined for testing a Seaside component. The `testComponentBehavior` method illustrates how to assert the behavior of the component under test, verifying its functionality.

Seaside offers an extensive set of advanced features and extensions that empower developers to build sophisticated web applications. By leveraging jQuery and Scriptaculous for dynamic content, supporting RESTful services, utilizing continuations for complex workflows, and employing the SUnit testing framework, developers can create robust, efficient, and user-friendly web applications in the Smalltalk environment.

Chapter 9

Advanced Object-Oriented Concepts in Smalltalk

Diving deeper into the object-oriented paradigm, this chapter addresses advanced concepts that underscore the versatility and strength of Smalltalk as an object-oriented programming language. It explores topics such as metaclasses, reflection, dynamic typing, and the implementation of complex design patterns within the Smalltalk framework. Additionally, the chapter delves into the utilization of traits for behavior reuse, strategies for multiple inheritance, and the application of protocols for enhancing code organization and readability. Armed with an understanding of these advanced concepts, readers will be positioned to leverage Smalltalk's full capabilities in designing sophisticated, modular, and highly reusable software architectures.

9.1 Introduction to Advanced OOP Concepts

Advancing in the exploration of Object-Oriented Programming (OOP) within Smalltalk necessitates a transition from foundational principles to more sophisticated concepts. This progression is essential for harnessing the full power of Smalltalk in solving complex software engineering problems. The advanced OOP concepts covered in this chapter provide the tools required for designing flexible, modular, and reusable software systems.

The cornerstone of OOP, encapsulation, is leveraged in more nuanced ways in advanced scenarios. Encapsulation not only ensures that objects maintain a well-defined interface by hiding their internal states and behaviors, but also facilitates the development of systems that are easier to maintain and extend.

- `Polymorphism`, another fundamental OOP concept, is revisited in this chapter with an emphasis on dynamic typing in Smalltalk. This feature supports the creation of more generic and flexible code, which can operate on objects of different classes without explicit knowledge of their specific types.
- `Inheritance` is further elaborated through the implementation of complex hierarchies that potentially include multiple inheritance and mixins. These mechanisms enable the sharing of code across different classes while preserving the unique characteristics of each class.

This section also introduces `metaclasses`, a powerful Smalltalk feature that allows classes themselves to be treated as objects. Understanding metaclasses is crucial for mastering Smalltalk's reflective capabilities, which enable programs to inspect and modify their own structure and behavior at runtime.

Reflection and introspection are closely examined, shedding light on the dynamic nature of Smalltalk. This dynamicity, coupled with advanced message passing and method lookup strategies, sets the stage for implementing sophisticated design patterns and architectural paradigms, such as Model-View-Controller (MVC).

Furthermore, the chapter discusses the strategic use of traits, a mechanism for composing classes from reusable units of behavior. Traits help overcome some of the limitations of single inheritance by enabling the shared use of methods across unrelated classes, significantly enhancing code reuse.

Multiple inheritance, often a source of complexity in OOP, is tackled through the use of mixins and trait-like structures in Smalltalk. This approach provides a clear pathway for combining behaviors from multiple sources without the common pitfalls associated with multiple inheritance.

In addition, protocols play a vital role in improving the organization and readability of code. By defining conventions for method naming and classification, protocols facilitate the development of more cohesive and easily navigable codebases.

The chapter concludes by exploring advanced topics such as dependency injection, inversion of control, object serialization, and robust API design. These concepts are pivotal for building scalable and maintainable applications that can cater to evolving business requirements.

This comprehensive overview sets the stage for a deep dive into each of these advanced object-oriented programming concepts, equipping the reader with the knowledge and skills necessary to fully exploit the power of Smalltalk in crafting sophisticated software architectures.

9.2 Understanding Metaclasses in Smalltalk

Metaclasses in Smalltalk embody a profound concept that underpins the language's uniform object model. Every class in Smalltalk is itself an instance of another class, known as a metaclass. This recursive relationship is central to the language's reflective capabilities and its dynamic nature. To grasp the significance of metaclasses, it is imperative to first understand the distinction between classes and instances, and then explore how metaclasses fit into this hierarchy.

A class in Smalltalk defines the structure and behavior of its instances. It specifies the instance variables and methods that the instances of the class will have. For example, consider a Person class with instance variables like name and age, and a method greet. Instances of the Person class will have their own name and age, and they can respond to the message greet. The Person class itself is an object, created from a metaclass, which we can refer to as Person class.

```
Person class >> name
    ^'Person'
```

Each class in Smalltalk, such as Person, is an instance of a unique metaclass. This metaclass is automatically generated by Smalltalk when a new class is defined. Although not typically manipulated directly by the programmer, metaclasses play an indispensable role in the language's flexibility and object model.

Metaclasses inherit from a special class called Class. This allows metaclass instances (which are classes themselves) to have methods that define class-level behavior. These methods are known as class methods. For instance, a method that returns the number of Person instances might be defined in the metaclass of Person.

```
Person class >> numberOfPeople
    ^PersonInstances size.
```

Moreover, metaclasses form a hierarchy that parallels the class hierarchy. If Employee is a subclass of Person, then Employee class is a subclass of Person class. This parallel hierarchy ensures that inheritance works uniformly for both instance methods and class methods.

```
Person class         Employee class
     |                     |
  Person               Employee
```

One of the most intriguing aspects of metaclasses is their contribution to the language's reflective capabilities. Since everything in Smalltalk is an object, including classes themselves, it is possible to examine and manipulate the class structure at runtime. This includes creating new classes, modifying existing ones, or querying the system for information about its classes - all of which are facilitated by metaclasses.

To illustrate, consider dynamically querying a class for its methods:

```
Person class methodDictionary keys.
```

This code snippet would return a collection of selector names representing all methods defined in the `Person` class.

In summary, metaclasses introduce a level of abstraction that unifies classes and objects under a single conceptual framework. They enable the dynamic features and reflective capabilities that make Smalltalk a highly expressive and malleable programming environment. Understanding metaclasses is crucial for leveraging the full power of Smalltalk's object-oriented model and for appreciating the elegance and depth of its design.

9.3 Reflection and Introspection: Exploring Smalltalk Objects

Reflection and introspection provide mechanisms for a program to inspect and modify itself at runtime. Smalltalk, renowned for its pure object-oriented approach, affords extensive support for these capabilities, making it a powerful tool for advanced programming techniques. This section elucidates the principles of reflection and introspection within the Smalltalk environment, demonstrating how these features can be leveraged to interrogate and manipulate objects, classes, and methods dynamically.

In Smalltalk, every entity is an object, including classes and methods. This uniformity allows for a consistent approach when using reflection and introspection to interact with the system. To commence with the exploration of these concepts, let us first distinguish between the two:

- **Reflection** refers to the ability of a program to manipulate the structure and behavior of objects at runtime. It includes actions such as creating new instances, invoking methods, and altering the class hierarchy.
- **Introspection**, on the other hand, is the process by which a program can examine the state and structure of objects at runtime without altering them. It encompasses querying an object about its class, properties, and methods.

Introspecting Objects

To demonstrate introspection in Smalltalk, consider the task of obtaining the class of an object. Smalltalk provides a simple yet powerful message, `class`, for this purpose. When sent to any object, it returns the object's class. Here is an example:

```
| sampleObject |
sampleObject := 'Hello, World!'.
Transcript show: sampleObject class name; cr.
```

In this example, we create a string object and send the `class` message to it. The result is then printed to the Transcript, showing that the object's class is `String`. The output is as follows:

```
String
```

Reflecting on Objects

When it comes to modifying objects and classes at runtime, reflection comes into play. For instance, to dynamically add a new method to a class, Smalltalk's `compile:` method can be used. Below is an illustrative example:

```
Object subclass: #MyClass
    instanceVariableNames: ''
    classVariableNames: ''
    poolDictionaries: ''
    category: 'MyCategory'.

MyClass compile: 'newMethod
```

```
    ^"This is a dynamically added method"'.

Transcript show: (MyClass new newMethod); cr.
```

Here, a new class named `MyClass` is defined under the category `MyCategory`. Then, the `compile:` method is used to dynamically add a new method named `newMethod` to `MyClass`. Finally, we instantiate `MyClass` and invoke the newly added method, which demonstrates reflection by dynamically altering the class's behavior. The output produced is:

```
This is a dynamically added method
```

Through reflection and introspection, Smalltalk programmers are equipped with powerful tools for dynamic code analysis and modification. These mechanisms not only facilitate the development of highly flexible and adaptable systems but also enable sophisticated metaprogramming techniques essential for advanced object-oriented programming.

In summary, reflection and introspection in Smalltalk empower developers with the capabilities to inspect and manipulate program structure and behavior at runtime. By understanding and utilizing these features, programmers can build more dynamic, robust, and versatile Smalltalk applications.

9.4 Dynamic Typing and Polymorphism Revisited

Dynamic typing and polymorphism are foundational concepts in Smalltalk, facilitating powerful design paradigms. In Smalltalk, the type of a variable is determined at runtime, unlike statically typed languages where it is fixed at compile time. This dynamic typing system adds flexibility but requires a thorough understanding to avoid runtime errors.

Polymorphism in Smalltalk is achieved through its dynamic typing system, allowing objects of different classes to be treated as objects of a single type as long as they adhere to a common interface. This principle is central to the concept of 'late binding' where method calls to an object are resolved at runtime, providing a high level of abstraction and flexibility in software design.

Dynamic Typing in Smalltalk

In Smalltalk, every variable is an object, and its type is not declared explicitly. For example, consider the following code snippet:

```
| myVariable |
myVariable := 123.
myVariable := 'A string object'.
```

In the code above, `myVariable` first references an integer object and later a string object. This illustrates how dynamic typing allows variables to reference objects of any class at runtime.

Dynamic typing enables the easy extension of programs but also poses challenges. Since type checking is performed at runtime, programming errors related to type mismatches may not surface until the code is executed. To mitigate this, Smalltalk programmers utilize rigorous testing strategies and leverage the powerful debugging tools provided by most Smalltalk environments.

Polymorphism Through Message Passing

Polymorphism is exemplified in Smalltalk through its message-passing mechanism. When a message (method call) is sent to an object, the Smalltalk runtime system determines at runtime which method to invoke based on the object's class. This mechanism allows objects of different classes to respond to the same message in their unique ways, as long as they implement the method.

Consider an example with a simple polymorphic scenario:

```
| duck mallard rubberDuck |
duck := Duck new.
mallard := Mallard new.
rubberDuck := RubberDuck new.

```

```
{duck, mallard, rubberDuck} do: [:eachDuck | eachDuck quack].
```

Here, `Duck`, `Mallard`, and `RubberDuck` could be different classes that implement the `quack` method. Despite their differences, each object in the collection responds to the `quack` message, demonstrating polymorphism.

Polymorphism and dynamic typing together allow Smalltalk developers to write more generic and reusable code. Functions or methods can operate on objects of various classes without needing to know the exact class of the objects at compile time, as long as the objects adhere to the expected interface.

To leverage these features effectively, understanding the principles of good object-oriented design is essential. Classes should be designed with clear, coherent responsibilities, and interfaces should be defined carefully to ensure that different objects can interoperate seamlessly.

In practice, Smalltalk's approach to dynamic typing and polymorphism encourages a design philosophy that emphasizes message-passing and object behavior over traditional type hierarchies. This leads to flexible and dynamic software systems that can be extended and modified with minimal changes to existing code, promoting the development of robust and maintainable software applications.

9.5 Message Passing and Method Lookup in Depth

In Smalltalk, the concept of message passing is fundamental. When a message is sent to an object, the system endeavors to find a method within the object's class that corresponds to the message. This process, known as method lookup, is at the core of Smalltalk's dynamic method dispatch mechanism.

The method lookup procedure follows a specific sequence:

1. The runtime system first checks the receiver object's class to see

if a method matching the message name exists.

2. If the method is found, it is executed. If not, the lookup process moves to the superclass of the current class and repeats the search.

3. This procedure continues up the inheritance hierarchy until the method is found or the topmost superclass is reached.

4. If the method is not found in any superclass, an error message is generated, signaling that the message is not understood.

This mechanism ensures that the most specific method relative to the receiver's class is selected for execution. The process of method lookup is made possible through the class hierarchy maintained in Smalltalk, which is facilitated by the use of metaclasses and the class-object relationship.

To illustrate, consider a Smalltalk class `Animal` with a subclass `Dog`. Assume `Dog` overrides a method named `makeSound`.

```
Animal subclass: #Dog
    instanceVariableNames: ''
    classVariableNames: ''
    poolDictionaries: ''
    category: 'Animals'.

Dog >> makeSound
    ^'Bark'.
```

When a `Dog` object receives the message `makeSound`, the system looks up the `Dog` class for the method. As it is found, the method returns the string 'Bark'.

```
| myDog |
myDog := Dog new.
Transcript show: myDog makeSound; cr.  % Outputs: Bark
```

The dynamic nature of Smalltalk's method lookup supports polymorphism, allowing objects of different classes to respond to the same message in different ways. It also underpins the flexibility of the language, allowing for runtime changes to classes and their methods.

In addition to standard method lookup, Smalltalk provides facilities for introspection and reflection, enabling programs to inquire about their structure and modify their behavior at runtime. This includes obtaining the list of methods a class supports, accessing the superclass of a class, and dynamically invoking methods by name.

For instance, to invoke the makeSound method dynamically, one could use:

```
| myDog sound |
myDog := Dog new.
sound := myDog perform: #makeSound.
Transcript show: sound; cr. % Similarly outputs: Bark
```

This capability facilitates advanced programming techniques, such as dependency injection, dynamic proxies, and aspect-oriented programming, which we will discuss in subsequent sections.

The message passing and method lookup mechanism in Smalltalk not only exemplifies the language's commitment to the principles of object orientation but also provides a flexible and powerful foundation for creating sophisticated, dynamically adaptable software systems.

9.6 Using Traits: Reusable Units of Behavior

Traits in Smalltalk are essentially reusable units of behavior that can be attached to classes. Unlike inheritance, which is a mechanism for defining an 'is-a' relationship, traits offer a way to compose classes out of reusable building blocks. This approach allows developers to avoid some of the complexities and limitations associated with multiple inheritance while still achieving a high degree of code reuse.

Defining Traits

A trait is defined in a manner similar to a class, but it only contains methods, not instance variables. The syntax for defining a trait in Smalltalk is illustrated below:

```
Trait named: #TraitName
   uses: {}
   category: 'CategoryName'
   methodDict: {
       #methodName -> (Method selector: #selector
                                  classified: 'MethodCategory'
                                  block: [ :args | method body ])
   }.
```

This example creates a trait named `TraitName` without using any other traits (as indicated by `uses: {}`), belonging to the category 'CategoryName', and it includes a single method defined in the dictionary `methodDict`.

Applying Traits to Classes

To apply a trait to a class, you use the `uses:` clause in the class definition. This clause accepts a trait composition expression, which can include the addition of traits and the exclusion of specific methods to resolve conflicts or provide custom implementations. The syntax is as follows:

```
Object subclass: #MyClass
   uses: TraitName
   instanceVariableNames: ''
   classVariableNames: ''
   poolDictionaries: ''
   category: 'CategoryName'.
```

In this example, `MyClass` applies the `TraitName` trait. This means that all the methods defined in `TraitName` are available in instances of `MyClass`, as if they were defined directly in the class.

Resolving Method Conflicts

When the same method is defined in multiple traits used by a class, a conflict arises. Smalltalk provides mechanisms for resolving these conflicts. One approach is to explicitly exclude conflicting methods from the trait composition and optionally provide a custom implementation directly in the class. The syntax for excluding a method from a trait is:

```
uses: TraitName - #methodName
```

This expression uses the trait `TraitName` but excludes the method `methodName`.

Advantages of Using Traits

Using traits offers several advantages:

- **Reusability:** Traits can be reused across different classes, promoting code reuse and reducing duplication.
- **Decoupling:** By separating behavior into traits, classes can be designed to be more focused and decoupled.
- **Conflict Resolution:** Traits provide mechanisms for resolving method conflicts, allowing for the safe composition of behavior from multiple sources.

While traits provide a powerful tool for organizing and reusing behavior, they are best used with a good understanding of the system's design and the interactions between classes. Applying traits judiciously can yield highly modular and maintainable code, leveraging the full capabilities of Smalltalk's object-oriented paradigm.

9.7 Multiple Inheritance and Mixins in Smalltalk

Multiple inheritance and the utilization of mixins represent substantial topics in the realm of object-oriented programming. Smalltalk, with its rich history and powerful object model, approaches these concepts with unique mechanisms that may at first appear unconventional to those familiar with other languages. This section elaborates on how multiple inheritance is addressed within Smalltalk and how mixins are effectively leveraged to enhance code reuse and modularity.

In traditional object-oriented languages, multiple inheritance allows a class to inherit behavior and attributes from more than one superclass. However, this can introduce complexity and ambiguity, particularly with the "diamond problem," where two superclasses share a common ancestor. Smalltalk resolves the potential issues arising from multiple inheritance by not supporting it directly in its class hierarchy. Instead, Smalltalk employs a single inheritance model.

Despite this, the need to reuse code and behaviors from multiple sources remains. Smalltalk's answer to this is the use of traits and mixins. A mixin in Smalltalk is a class that is intended to provide additional functionality to other classes not by means of inheritance but through composition. This allows for a level of flexibility in code reuse and optimization that multiple inheritance seeks to provide but without its associated complexities.

Mixins in Smalltalk

A mixin is essentially a class that is designed to be injected into another class, thereby acting as a supplementary source of methods. Unlike traditional classes, mixins do not typically instantiate objects; instead, their purpose is to augment the behavior of other classes. To illustrate this, consider the following example:

```
Object subclass: #Shape
    instanceVariableNames: ''
    classVariableNames: ''
    poolDictionaries: ''
    category: 'Shapes'.

Shape subclass: #Rectangle
    instanceVariableNames: 'width height'
    classVariableNames: ''
    poolDictionaries: ''
    category: 'Shapes'.

Rectangle mixin: #ColorMixin.
```

In the above example, `Rectangle` is a subclass of `Shape`, and we want to add color functionality to our `Rectangle` objects without altering the existing class hierarchy. We achieve this by creating a `ColorMixin` that contains the color-related methods and then injecting this mixin into the `Rectangle` class. This technique enables `Rectangle` to possess both its intrinsic properties and the additional capabilities provided by `ColorMixin`.

Benefits of Using Mixins

The advantages of utilizing mixins in Smalltalk are manifold. Here are some key benefits:

- **Enhanced Modularity**: Mixins allow for a highly modular approach to code organization. Functionalities can be encapsulated within mixins and then selectively applied to classes that require them.
- **Code Reuse**: By abstracting functionalities into mixins, there's a significant reduction in code duplication. The same mixin can be applied to multiple classes, fostering code reuse.
- **Flexibility**: Mixins offer a flexible way to extend the behavior of classes without altering the class hierarchy. This is particularly useful in scenarios where modifying the inheritance chain is not feasible or desirable.
- **Separation of Concerns**: With mixins, it's easier to maintain a clear separation of concerns. Each mixin can focus on providing a specific functionality, making the codebase more comprehensible and maintainable.

While Smalltalk does not support multiple inheritance directly, it provides a powerful alternative through the use of mixins. This approach not only circumvents the complexities associated with multiple inheritance but also offers a flexible, modular, and reusable mechanism for extending class functionality. By effectively leveraging mixins, Smalltalk developers can achieve a high degree of code reuse and modularity, crucial aspects in the design of sophisticated software systems.

9.8 Design Patterns in Smalltalk: Implementing Model-View-Controller (MVC)

In this section, we will discuss the Model-View-Controller (MVC) design pattern, which is pivotal for developing applications with a clean separation of concerns. This pattern divides the application into three interconnected components, thereby making it easier to manage and update. The implementation of MVC in Smalltalk not only exemplifies Smalltalk's robustness in handling object-oriented concepts but also showcases its capability to accommodate complex design patterns.

Model

The Model represents the application's data structure, along with the business logic. In Smalltalk, an object-oriented language, the Model is implemented as a class or a group of classes that encapsulate the data and the behaviors associated with that data.

```
Object subclass: #BankAccount
    instanceVariableNames: 'balance'
    classVariableNames: ''
    poolDictionaries: ''
    category: 'Financial-Models'.

BankAccount >> initialize
    balance := 0.
```

In the above example, `BankAccount` acts as a model, holding the balance as its state and able to perform various operations like deposits and withdrawals.

View

The View component is responsible for presenting the data to the user. It observes the Model and updates its presentation when the Model changes. Smalltalk utilizes its powerful graphical libraries to implement Views. A simple View might display the balance of BankAccount.

```
Object subclass: #BankAccountView
    instanceVariableNames: 'account displayLabel'
    classVariableNames: ''
    poolDictionaries: ''
    category: 'Financial-Views'.

BankAccountView >> displayBalance
    displayLabel contents: account balance printString.
```

Here, `BankAccountView` maintains a reference to a `BankAccount` instance (the Model) and a `displayLabel` for showing the balance. The `displayBalance` method updates `displayLabel` with the account's current balance.

Controller

The Controller acts as an intermediary between the Model and the View. It listens to events generated by the View and processes them, which sometimes result in updates to the Model. In Smalltalk, Controllers are implemented as subclasses of `Controller` or `Object` class, equipped with event-handling capabilities.

```
Object subclass: #BankAccountController
    instanceVariableNames: 'view'
    classVariableNames: ''
    poolDictionaries: ''
    category: 'Financial-Controllers'.

BankAccountController >> deposit: anAmount
    view account deposit: anAmount.
    view displayBalance.
```

In the provided code snippet, `BankAccountController` responds to deposit operations. It updates the `BankAccount` (Model) through the `View` and triggers the `View` to refresh the account balance display.

Putting it All Together: MVC in Action

Integrating the Model, View, and Controller into a functioning MVC pattern involves ensuring that the View is aware of changes to the

Model and that the Controller can respond to user inputs or other events by updating the Model, which in turn, reflects in the View. In Smalltalk, this is facilitated through its message-passing framework and the use of observers or dependents.

```
| account view controller |
account := BankAccount new.
view := BankAccountView new.
controller := BankAccountController new.

view account: account.
controller view: view.

controller deposit: 100.
```

In the final arrangement, an instance of `BankAccount`, `BankAccountView`, and `BankAccountController` are created and linked together. The `deposit:` method on the `controller` is called to simulate a deposit action, demonstrating how the MVC components interact within Smalltalk.

To summarize, the MVC design pattern in Smalltalk exemplifies a clean separation of concerns—where the Model encapsulates core data and behavior, the View handles data presentation and user interaction, and the Controller mediates input and updates models. This separation facilitates maintenance, enhances scalability, and supports modularity in application development.

9.9 The Role of Protocols in Object Orientation

Protocols in object-oriented programming, particularly within the context of Smalltalk, serve as a vital means of defining a set of methods that a class must or can implement. Smalltalk, known for its pure object-oriented approach, leverages protocols to enhance code organization, readability, and interoperability among objects. This discusses the significance of protocols, how they are used in Smalltalk, and their impact on the development of robust, modular software.

In Smalltalk, a protocol is not a language construct but a convention used to group methods related by functionality within a class. This grouping aids in understanding the capabilities of a class at a glance and ensures that classes adhering to the same protocol can be used interchangeably insofar as the protocol's functionality is concerned. This concept is akin to interfaces in languages like Java but implemented through naming conventions and documentation rather than explicit language features.

Let's explore the mechanism of defining and utilizing protocols in Smalltalk with an example. Consider a protocol named `Serializable`, intended to be used by any class whose instances need to be serialized into a string format for storage or network transmission.

```
Object subclass: #MySerializableClass
    instanceVariableNames: ''
    classVariableNames: ''
    poolDictionaries: ''
    category: 'MyCategory'.

MySerializableClass class>>protocol: 'Serializable'
    ^#(serialize deserialize)
```

In the snippet above, the class `MySerializableClass` is defined with a class method `protocol:` that returns an array of method selectors (`serialize` and `deserialize`), indicating the methods that belong to the `Serializable` protocol. This approach does not enforce protocol adherence at compile time but serves as a clear documentation tool and guideline for developers.

Adhering to a protocol means implementing all the methods that the protocol entails. For classes that comply with the `Serializable` protocol, here is an example implementation:

```
MySerializableClass>>serialize
    "Converts the receiving object into a string representation."
    ^self printString.

MySerializableClass>>deserialize: aString
    "Recreates an instance of the class from a string representation."
    "This is a simplistic implementation for illustrative purposes."
    ^self new initializeFromString: aString.
```

With this in place, any object of `MySerializableClass` can now be serialized and deserialized using the defined methods. The use of protocols ensures that any other class intending to be serializable can implement these methods, thereby adhering to the `Serializable` protocol. This drastically improves code reuse and readability, as developers can easily identify classes that fulfill specific roles within the application.

Moreover, protocols enhance polymorphism in Smalltalk. Since Smalltalk is a dynamically typed language, the actual class of an object matters less at runtime than the messages it can respond to - a core principle of duck typing. By organizing methods into protocols, developers can design systems that rely on the presence of behavior rather than specific class hierarchies, enhancing flexibility and decoupling in the software design.

In summary, protocols play a crucial role in organizing and defining the behaviors that classes should implement in Smalltalk. While not enforced by the compiler, protocols serve as a powerful documentation tool and guideline for developing consistent, modular, and reusable code. Their use facilitates a high degree of polymorphism and code reuse, pivotal in crafting flexible, robust software architectures.

9.10 Dependency Injection and Inversion of Control

Dependency Injection (DI) and Inversion of Control (IoC) are pivotal concepts in modern software design, particularly within the realm of object-oriented programming. Smalltalk, with its dynamic nature and strong emphasis on objects, provides a fertile ground for applying these principles. DI and IoC contribute significantly to making software systems more modular, flexible, and maintainable.

Dependency Injection is a design pattern that allows a class's dependencies to be injected into it at runtime rather than the class creating them itself. This approach decouples the instantiation of a class's dependencies from its business logic, making the class easier to manage and test.

Let's consider a simple example to illustrate DI in Smalltalk. Suppose we have two classes: `EmailClient` and `SMTPService`. Without DI, an instance of `SMTPService` might be created directly within `EmailClient`, tightly coupling the two classes. With DI, `EmailClient` would receive an instance of `SMTPService` (or an interface it conforms to) through its initializer or through a setter method.

```
EmailClient >> initializeWithService: aService
    SMTPService := aService.
```

This approach decouples the `EmailClient` from the concrete implementation of the SMTP service, increasing the modularity of the application and simplifying unit testing.

Inversion of Control, on the other hand, refers to the inversion of the flow of control seen in traditional procedural programming. In an IoC scenario, the high-level module dictates when and what from the low-level modules will be executed or invoked. Smalltalk's highly dynamic environment and its messaging system naturally facilitate IoC through techniques such as dependency injection, event notification systems, and the use of strategy patterns.

To clarify, consider an application that responds to user inputs with various actions. Without IoC, each input would directly call the respective action code, leading to a rigid and less manageable codebase. Implementing IoC, the application could instead dispatch user inputs to a central controller that then selects the appropriate action. This decouples the input handling from the action performance logic, making the application more flexible.

One of the main benefits of applying DI and IoC in Smalltalk applications is an enhancement in the testability of code. By injecting mocks or stubs of complex objects, testing becomes more focused on the behavior of the class under test, rather than its dependencies. Additionally, these patterns promote a design that adheres to the Single Responsibility Principle, as objects delegate tasks outside their core functionalities to dependencies, which can be swapped easily.

However, while DI and IoC offer numerous advantages, they also introduce complexity into the system. It becomes paramount to manage dependencies carefully to avoid issues such as runtime errors due to missing dependencies or the overuse of IoC containers, which can lead to so-called "injection sprawls".

```
Example Output:
- A decoupled class architecture improving maintainability
- Easier unit testing through mock or stub implementations
```

Dependency Injection and Inversion of Control represent advanced techniques in the object-oriented paradigm that hold the key to building highly flexible, decoupled, and manageable software architectures in Smalltalk. By understanding and correctly applying these concepts, developers can significantly enhance the quality and longevity of their Smalltalk applications.

9.11 Advanced Object Serialization Techniques

Serialization in Smalltalk is a process that converts objects into a stream of bytes, enabling them to be stored or transmitted over a network. Conversely, deserialization rebuilds the object from the stream. This section delves into advanced techniques for serialization in Smalltalk, focusing on custom serialization strategies, serialization of complex object graphs, and handling of cyclic dependencies.

Smalltalk's flexible nature allows the implementation of custom serialization mechanisms tailored to specific requirements. Below is an example illustrating how to define custom serialization for a class.

```
Object subclass: #MyClass
    instanceVariableNames: 'name age'
    classVariableNames: ''
    poolDictionaries: ''
    category: 'MyCategory'.

MyClass>>serialize
    | stream |
```

```
    stream := WriteStream on: String new.
    stream nextPutAll: self name; nextPut: $; nextPutAll: self age printString.
    ^stream contents
```

The method `serialize` customizes the serialization process for instances of `MyClass`. It concatenates the name and age of the instance, separated by a semicolon, and returns the resulting string.

Serialization of complex objects and object graphs involves traversing references and serializing each object encountered. Smalltalk provides utilities to simplify this process, but handling cyclic references requires additional care to avoid infinite loops. An approach to detect cycles is to keep a registry of already serialized objects.

```
serializeObject: anObject
    | serializedObjects stream |
    serializedObjects := Dictionary new.
    stream := WriteStream on: String new.

    self innerSerialize: anObject
        on: stream
        with: serializedObjects.
    ^stream contents

innerSerialize: anObject on: aStream with: serializedObjects
    | reference |
    (serializedObjects includesKey: anObject) ifTrue:
        [^aStream nextPutAll: '(cyclic reference)'].
    serializedObjects at: anObject put: true.
    reference := anObject references.
    reference do: [:each | self innerSerialize: each
                                   on: aStream
                                   with: serializedObjects].
```

The above code snippets illustrate a recursive strategy to serialize an object graph while managing cyclic references. The dictionary `serializedObjects` serves as a registry to track which objects have been serialized.

Another important aspect is the serialization of collection objects. Smalltalk collections may comprise diverse elements requiring individual serialization methods. Iterating over the collection and invoking the appropriate serialization method for each element is necessary.

```
serializeCollection: aCollection
    | stream |
    stream := WriteStream on: String new.
```

```
    aCollection do: [:each |
        stream nextPutAll: (self serializeObject: each); nextPut: $.].
    ^stream contents
```

This method iterates over every element in aCollection, serializes it, and appends it to the stream, separated by periods.

Serialization plays a vital role in persistence, network communication, and deep copying of objects. Advanced serialization techniques, as discussed, enhance the capability to manage complex serialization scenarios, enabling efficient and effective object serialization in Smalltalk applications.

9.12 Designing Robust APIs in Smalltalk

Designing robust Application Programming Interfaces (APIs) in Smalltalk requires a deep understanding of both the language's capabilities and the principles that underpin effective API design. This section will discuss the key considerations and best practices that should guide the development of APIs in Smalltalk, ensuring they are both powerful and easy to use.

Firstly, the principle of clarity in API design cannot be overstated. An API's usability significantly depends on how clear and intuitive its interface is. In Smalltalk, this often means leveraging the language's readability and simplicity. For instance, method names should be descriptive and clearly convey their function. Consider the difference between a method named `add:` versus one named `addElement:`. The latter offers a more explicit indication of its purpose, which is to add an element to a collection.

```
collection addElement: anElement.
```

Secondly, consistency is crucial in API design. Consistency in naming conventions, parameter ordering, and error handling can significantly reduce the learning curve for new users of the API. Smalltalk's highly readable syntax can be a boon here, as it naturally encourages a more conversational and thus consistent approach to method naming and parameter usage. For example, if a set of collection manipulation methods starts with `add`, `remove`, `find`, ensure that similar methods in different parts of the API adhere to this pattern.

Thirdly, the use of polymorphism in Smalltalk allows for flexible and adaptive API design. When designing APIs that interact with various types of objects, polymorphism can be used to ensure that methods behave appropriately regardless of the specific type of the object they are dealing with. This can reduce the need for type checking and casting, leading to a cleaner and more elegant API design.

```
aCollection do: [:each | each process].
```

Here, `process` can be a method implemented in multiple classes differently, allowing `aCollection` to hold objects of different types, with each responding to `process` in its way.

Fourthly, Smalltalk's dynamic nature and its powerful reflection capabilities offer unique opportunities for advanced API design. Methods can be generated or modified at runtime, allowing for highly adaptive and responsive APIs that can adjust their behavior based on the application's current context or state. While powerful, this capability should be used judiciously, as overly dynamic APIs can become hard to understand and debug.

```
MyClass compile: 'newMethod ^42'.
(MyClass new newMethod) "This will return 42"
```

Fifthly, error handling in Smalltalk APIs emphasizes clarity and recoverability. Smalltalk's exception system allows for precise control over error conditions, enabling APIs to fail gracefully and provide meaningful feedback to the user. API methods should therefore be designed with clear error conditions and helpful error messages, leveraging Smalltalk's exceptions to facilitate error diagnosis and recovery.

```
[myApiMethod] on: Error do: [:ex | Transcript show: ex messageText].
```

Here, any error raised by `myApiMethod` will be caught, and its message displayed to the user, allowing for more informative and user-friendly error handling.

Lastly, documentation plays a key role in the usability of an API. Smalltalk's literate programming capabilities, where documentation and code can be interspersed, should be fully utilized to create comprehensive, example-rich API documentation. This not only aids in understanding the API's purpose and usage but also helps in maintaining it over time.

```
"Example usage of myApiMethod"
myApi collection: aCollection addElement: anElement.
```

In summary, designing robust APIs in Smalltalk involves a deep commitment to clarity, consistency, flexibility, and user-friendliness. By adhering to these principles, leveraging Smalltalk's unique features, and maintaining comprehensive documentation, API developers can create powerful, intuitive, and adaptable interfaces that stand the test of time.

9.13 Best Practices for Advanced Object-Oriented Design

Object-oriented design (OOD) principles are foundational to creating effective, maintainable, and scalable software. In the context of Smalltalk, these principles take on a unique significance due to the language's pure object-oriented nature and dynamic capabilities. This section elucidates several best practices tailored for advanced object-oriented design within the Smalltalk environment.

Embrace Encapsulation Fully

Encapsulation is a cornerstone of object-oriented programming, promoting modular design by hiding internal state and behavior from the outside world. In Smalltalk, all interactions with an object occur through message passing, inherently enforcing encapsulation. However, to truly leverage this, it is crucial to expose only what is necessary through an object's interface. Consider minimizing public accessors and mutators (getters and setters), and instead focus on providing methods that perform meaningful operations on the object's data.

```
Object subclass: #BankAccount
   instanceVariableNames: 'balance'
   classVariableNames: ''
   poolDictionaries: ''
   category: 'Financial-Models'.

BankAccount >> initializeWithBalance: initialBalance
   balance := initialBalance.

BankAccount >> deposit: anAmount
   balance := balance + anAmount.

BankAccount >> withdraw: anAmount
   balance := balance - anAmount.
```

In the above example, rather than providing direct access to the `balance` variable, deposit and withdraw methods are provided to manipulate the account balance safely.

Adhere to the Liskov Substitution Principle

The Liskov Substitution Principle (LSP) posits that objects of a superclass should be replaceable with objects of a subclass without affecting the correctness of the program. In Smalltalk, where polymorphism and dynamic typing are extensively utilized, adhering to LSP ensures that subclassing is used appropriately to extend or modify behavior without introducing errors.

```
Object subclass: #Shape
   instanceVariableNames: ''
   classVariableNames: ''
   poolDictionaries: ''
   category: 'Shapes'.

Shape >> area
   ^self subclassResponsibility.

Rectangle subclass: #Rectangle
   instanceVariableNames: 'width height'
   classVariableNames: ''
   poolDictionaries: ''
   category: 'Shapes'.
```

```

Rectangle >> area
    ^width * height.
```

In the example, any `Shape` can be substituted with a `Rectangle` without altering the ability to calculate the area, complying with LSP.

Maximize Reuse with Inheritance and Composition

Inheritance and composition are powerful mechanisms for reuse in object-oriented design. Smalltalk's flexible class hierarchy and dynamic messaging facilitate both, but choosing when to use each is vital for creating a maintainable design.

Prefer composition over inheritance when the relationship can be described as "has-a" rather than "is-a". Composition offers greater flexibility and reduces the tight coupling that can occur with extensive use of inheritance.

Design for Testability

Creating software that is easy to test is critical for maintaining its reliability and robustness. In Smalltalk, leverage the dynamism of the environment to write tests that can mock dependencies and isolate units of code effectively.

```
TestCase subclass: #BankAccountTest
    instanceVariableNames: 'account'
    classVariableNames: ''
    poolDictionaries: ''
    category: 'Financial-Models-Tests'.

BankAccountTest >> setUp
    account := BankAccount initializeWithBalance: 100.

BankAccountTest >> testDeposit
    account deposit: 50.
    self assert: (account balance) equals: 150.
```

The `setUp` method initializes the conditions for each test, ensuring that tests run in isolation and are repeatable, a hallmark of a testable design.

Leverage Smalltalk's Dynamic Environment

Smalltalk's reflective capabilities and dynamic environment offer unique opportunities for advanced object-oriented design, such as dynamic method creation, introspection, and late binding. These features allow for designs that can adapt at runtime, offering unprecedented flexibility. Caution is advised, however, to avoid complexity that could undermine understandability and maintainability.

```
Rectangle >> setWidth: w height: h
    width := w.
    height := h.
    self changed: #area.
```

In this mock example, a `Rectangle` object could notify observers of a change in its area, leveraging Smalltalk's dynamic message passing to implement observer patterns elegantly.

Advanced object-oriented design in Smalltalk benefits from adhering to solid OOD principles while taking full advantage of the language's capabilities. Encapsulation, adherence to the Liskov Substitution Principle, thoughtful use of inheritance and composition, designing for testability, and making use of Smalltalk's dynamic features form the cornerstone of sophisticated, robust, and reusable designs.

Chapter 10

Optimizing Smalltalk Performance and Memory Management

Optimizing performance and managing memory efficiently are crucial for developing scalable and responsive applications in Smalltalk. This chapter delves into methodologies and best practices for enhancing the speed and efficiency of Smalltalk programs. Readers will learn about profiling tools for identifying bottlenecks, techniques for optimizing message passing and collection handling, as well as strategies for effective garbage collection and memory allocation. Furthermore, it covers advanced aspects such as just-in-time (JIT) compilation and virtual machine (VM) tuning. Equipped with this knowledge, developers will be able to fine-tune their Smalltalk applications for optimal performance and resource management.

10.1 Introduction to Performance Optimization in Smalltalk

Performance optimization in Smalltalk encompasses a range of techniques designed to improve the execution speed and efficiency of Smalltalk programs. As a dynamically typed, object-oriented programming language, Smalltalk provides immense flexibility and expressiveness, allowing developers to create complex applications with less code. However, this flexibility can come at the cost of performance. Efficiently managing memory and optimizing code execution are essential for developing scalable and responsive Smalltalk applications. This section will discuss the fundamental concepts and methodologies for performance optimization in Smalltalk, setting the stage for more detailed explorations in the subsequent sections.

Smalltalk's performance can be significantly influenced by how objects send messages to each other, how memory is allocated and managed, and how the garbage collector operates. Understanding these aspects is crucial for identifying bottlenecks and implementing effective optimizations. Let's explore the key areas that impact Smalltalk's performance:

- **Message Passing:** Unlike static languages, Smalltalk performs message passing at runtime, which can add overhead to method invocations. Optimizing how messages are passed can lead to substantial performance improvements.
- **Memory Allocation:** Objects in Smalltalk are dynamically allocated in memory. Efficient management of this memory allocation can minimize overhead and improve application responsiveness.
- **Garbage Collection:** Smalltalk's automated garbage collection helps manage memory by freeing up space occupied by objects no longer in use. Optimizing garbage collection routines can prevent performance degradation, especially in applications that create and destroy many objects.

- **Collections Handling:** Smalltalk's powerful collection classes are central to the language. Enhancing the performance of operations on collections can have a dramatic effect on the overall performance of an application.

To lay the groundwork for performance optimization, it is also important to understand the tools and techniques available for profiling Smalltalk applications. Profiling allows developers to identify the parts of their application that are the most resource-intensive, providing a targeted approach to optimization. Techniques such as method tracing and sampling can be used to gather insights into an application's performance characteristics.

In summary, optimizing performance in Smalltalk involves a holistic approach that includes reducing the overhead of message passing, managing memory allocation and garbage collection efficiently, and optimizing operations on collections. Armed with the right knowledge and tools, developers can significantly enhance the speed and efficiency of their Smalltalk applications. The subsequent sections will dive deeper into each of these areas, providing specific strategies and best practices for performance optimization in Smalltalk.

10.2 Understanding Smalltalk's Memory Model

In this section, we will discuss Smalltalk's memory model, an essential component for optimizing the performance and managing the memory of Smalltalk applications effectively. Smalltalk's memory model is characterized by its simplicity and dynamism, which, while facilitating ease of programming and making dynamic features straightforward to implement, presents unique challenges in terms of memory management and performance optimization.

Smalltalk applications operate within an environment known as the Smalltalk virtual machine (VM), which abstracts the underlying hardware and operating system to provide a consistent runtime environment across different platforms. The VM employs a managed memory model, handling memory allocation and deallocation automatically through a mechanism known as garbage collection. However, understanding the nuances of this memory model enables developers to write more memory-efficient code and to debug memory-related issues more effectively.

Objects and Memory Allocation

In Smalltalk, everything is an object, including simple values such as numbers and characters, complex data structures, and even code blocks. When an object is created, the VM allocates memory for it on the heap. This allocation is transparent to the developer, emphasizing the language's high level of abstraction. However, the way objects are allocated and referenced has implications for memory usage and application performance.

Each object in Smalltalk occupies a contiguous block of memory. The size of this block depends on the object's type and its contents. For instance, an integer may occupy less space than a collection object containing multiple items. Understanding these differences is crucial for optimizing memory usage, especially when working with large datasets or complex data structures.

Garbage Collection

Garbage collection (GC) is a fundamental aspect of Smalltalk's memory model. The GC process is responsible for identifying and reclaiming memory occupied by objects that are no longer accessible or needed by the application. Smalltalk's garbage collector typically operates in a "stop-the-world" manner, meaning that it pauses the application's execution to perform the collection. Although this can impact performance, especially in memory-intensive applications, modern Smalltalk VMs employ various strategies to minimize the disruption, including incremental and generational garbage collection techniques.

Memory Segmentation and Compaction

The Smalltalk VM organizes the heap memory into segments to optimize memory allocation and garbage collection. These segments help manage memory more efficiently by grouping related objects together and reducing fragmentation. Memory fragmentation occurs when the heap is filled with small blocks of free space between allocated objects, making it difficult to find contiguous blocks of memory for new objects. To mitigate this, the VM periodically performs a process called compaction, which rearranges objects in memory to consolidate free space into larger contiguous blocks.

Weak References

Smalltalk provides a mechanism for creating weak references, which allows the developer to reference an object without preventing it from being garbage-collected. This feature is particularly useful for implementing caches and managing large objects that may not always be needed. A weak reference does not count as a regular reference in the eyes of the garbage collector, so when the only remaining references to an object are weak, the object can be collected to free memory.

Mastering Smalltalk's memory model involves understanding how objects are allocated, managed, and reclaimed by the VM. By leveraging knowledge of garbage collection, memory segmentation, and weak references, developers can write more memory-efficient applications and tackle memory-related performance issues more effectively.

10.3 Profiling Smalltalk Applications: Tools and Techniques

Profiling is an essential step in optimizing the performance of Smalltalk applications. It involves measuring various aspects of program execution, such as time spent in functions, number of method calls, and memory usage, to identify bottlenecks and areas that require optimization.

Understanding Profiling Concepts

Before diving into specific tools, it is important to understand two key concepts in profiling: sampling and instrumentation. Sampling involves periodically checking which part of the code is being executed and recording statistics, whereas instrumentation modifies the code to insert measurement code, which directly measures the behavior of the program.

Tools for Profiling Smalltalk Applications

Several tools are available for profiling Smalltalk applications, each with its own methodology and focus. Some popular options include the MessageTally, TimeProfileBrowser, and MemoryUsage tools provided within various Smalltalk environments.

- `MessageTally` is a tool that uses sampling to provide an overview of time spent in method executions. It is particularly useful for identifying methods that consume a significant amount of CPU time.

- `TimeProfileBrowser` offers more detailed profiling data, including the number of method executions and the time spent in each. It's instrumental in pinpointing performance bottlenecks at the method level.

- `MemoryUsage` tools are specialized in tracking memory allocation and identifying potential memory leaks or inefficient memory use. They are essential for managing memory effectively in Smalltalk applications.

Profiling Techniques

Effective profiling involves more than just running tools; it also requires applying certain techniques to ensure meaningful and actionable insights.

1. Start by profiling the entire application to get a general sense of where bottlenecks might be. This will guide you on where to focus for more detailed profiling.

2. Use `MessageTally` to identify methods that are frequent or time-consuming, then drill down with `TimeProfileBrowser` for a detailed examination of these methods.

3. Pay attention to memory usage patterns. If certain operations cause unexpected spikes in memory use, investigate further using memory profiling tools.

4. Iterate on profiling and optimization. Optimize identified hotspots, then re-profile to measure improvements and detect new bottlenecks.

Interpreting Profiling Data

Once profiling data is collected, the next step is to analyze and interpret this information to make optimization decisions.

1. For CPU profiling, focus on methods with the highest execution time or call count. These are potential candidates for optimization, such as through algorithm improvements or caching.

2. In memory profiling, look for patterns of excessive allocation or objects that are not being released, indicating potential memory leaks.

3. Compare pre- and post-optimization profiling results to confirm that performance has indeed improved and to ensure that no new bottlenecks have been introduced.

Best Practices for Profiling

Finally, adhering to a set of best practices can make profiling more effective:

- Profile in an environment that closely resembles production to obtain realistic results.
- Prioritize optimizations based on profiling data, focusing on the most impactful changes first.
- Avoid premature optimization; profile regularly as part of the development cycle, particularly after significant changes or additions to the codebase.
- Use profiling data to inform decisions, but also keep broader design considerations in mind.

Proficient use of profiling tools and techniques is fundamental to optimizing Smalltalk applications. By identifying performance bottlenecks and inefficient memory use, developers can make targeted optimizations, leading to faster and more efficient applications.

10.4 Optimizing Message Passing for Performance

Optimizing message passing in Smalltalk is fundamental for enhancing the performance of applications. Smalltalk's programming environment is highly dynamic, where message passing is a core part of its object-oriented paradigm. Efficient message passing can lead to significant improvements in execution speed and application responsiveness. This section will dissect strategies for optimizing message passing, including the use of inline caching, selective message inlining, and dynamic message optimization.

Inline Caching

Inline caching is a technique that aims to reduce the overhead associated with method lookup in dynamic languages like Smalltalk. Every time a message is sent to an object, Smalltalk's runtime environment must locate the appropriate method to execute. This lookup process can be time-consuming, especially in applications with a high volume of message sends. Inline caching mitigates this overhead by caching the results of method lookups.

The following example demonstrates the implementation of a basic inline cache in Smalltalk:

```
Smalltalk at: #Rectangle put: (Object subclass: #Rectangle
    instanceVariableNames: 'width height'
    classVariableNames: ''
    poolDictionaries: ''
    category: 'Shapes').

Rectangle class>>newWithWidth: w height: h
    ^self new initializeWithWidth: w height: h.

Rectangle>>initializeWithWidth: w height: h
    width := w.
    height := h.

Rectangle>>area
    ^width * height.
```

In the example above, a `Rectangle` class is defined with methods for setting dimensions and calculating the area. Without optimization, every call to `area` would involve a method lookup. An inline cache reduces this overhead by remembering the method's location from previous calls.

Selective Message Inlining

Another effective optimization technique is selective message inlining, which involves replacing frequently called methods with their body's code. This reduces the overhead of message passing by eliminating the need for method lookup and context switching.

Consider the `Rectangle` class example. It's clear that the `area` method could be called frequently. By inlining the `area` method's code directly where it is called, the overhead can be significantly reduced.

Dynamic Message Optimization

Dynamic message optimization refers to the runtime adaptation of message passing mechanisms based on execution patterns. Smalltalk VMs can monitor which messages are sent frequently and apply optimizations such as inline caching and method inlining dynamically.

For instance, suppose a particular message send pattern is detected where the `area` method of the `Rectangle` class is called repeatedly in a loop. In such a scenario, the VM might automatically apply inline caching or selective inlining specifically for this message send pattern, thus optimizing performance without requiring explicit code changes.

Optimizing message passing in Smalltalk involves a multi-pronged approach, incorporating inline caching, selective message inlining, and dynamic message optimization. By leveraging these techniques, developers can significantly improve the speed and efficiency of their Smalltalk applications. It is worth noting, however, that these optimizations should be applied judiciously, taking into consideration the readability and maintainability of the code.

10.5 Memory Management: Garbage Collection and Manual Tuning

Effective memory management is central to the performance of Smalltalk programs. In Smalltalk, memory management encompasses garbage collection and manual tuning strategies that ensure optimal use of resources, minimizing memory leaks and improving application responsiveness. This section will discuss the mechanisms of garbage collection in Smalltalk, manual memory tuning techniques, and their applicability in real-world scenarios.

Understanding Garbage Collection in Smalltalk

Garbage collection (GC) in Smalltalk is an automatic memory management feature that reclaims memory occupied by objects that are no longer accessible or needed by the program. Smalltalk's garbage collector predominantly operates on a generational garbage collection model. This model categorizes objects based on their age and allocates them into two main spaces: young and old generations.

Generational Garbage Collection Model

In the generational garbage collection model, most objects are allocated in the young generation space, where they reside until they become unreachable or survive multiple garbage collection cycles. Objects that persist are then promoted to the old generation space. This separation is predicated on the hypothesis that "most objects die young," which makes frequent, minor collections in the young generation space more efficient than conducting less frequent, but major, collections in the old generation.

Garbage Collection Phases

The garbage collection process in Smalltalk involves several phases:

- *Marking*: Identifying live objects that are still accessible from root references.
- *Sweeping*: Reclaiming the memory of objects that are not marked as live.
- *Compacting* (optional): Consolidating free memory spaces to address fragmentation, applicable primarily in the old generation space.

The efficacy of garbage collection in Smalltalk can significantly impact application performance. Excessive garbage creation and collection can lead to frequent GC pauses, affecting the responsiveness of the application. Therefore, understanding and optimizing garbage collection processes are crucial.

Manual Tuning of Memory Usage

While garbage collection automates memory management, developers can employ manual tuning techniques to optimize memory usage further. These techniques involve managing the lifecycle of objects, reducing memory footprint, and optimizing object allocation and retention strategies.

Reducing Memory Footprint

One effective approach to manual memory tuning is minimizing the memory footprint of the application. This can involve:

- Reducing the size of objects, by optimizing data structures or choosing more space-efficient data types.
- Limiting the scope and duration of object retention to reduce the longevity of objects unnecessarily occupying space in memory.
- Using object pools for frequently used objects to avoid constant allocation and deallocation, which can lead to fragmentation.

Object Allocation and Retention

Optimizing object allocation involves strategies such as:

- Delaying the creation of objects until they are truly needed (lazy initialization).
- Reusing objects wherever possible instead of creating new instances.

Careful management of object retention, on the other hand, involves ensuring that objects are released when they are no longer needed. Unnecessary retention of objects can lead to memory leaks, where memory is consumed by objects that are no longer part of the active workflow of the application but are still not collected by the garbage collector due to lingering references.

Effective memory management in Smalltalk, through a combination of automated garbage collection and manual tuning, is critical for developing applications that are both efficient and scalable. By understanding the underlying principles of garbage collection and employing manual memory optimization techniques, developers can significantly enhance the performance and responsiveness of their Smalltalk applications.

10.6 Optimizing Collections and Loops

Optimizing collections and loops in Smalltalk is a significant aspect of enhancing the performance of Smalltalk applications. Efficient use of collections and loops not only speeds up the execution time but also contributes to better memory management. In this section, we shall explore various techniques and best practices for optimizing the performance of collections and loops.

Improving Loop Efficiency

Loops are fundamental constructs in programming used to repeat a block of code multiple times. However, inefficient loop constructs can lead to performance bottlenecks. Here are strategies for improving loop efficiency in Smalltalk:

- Utilize collection operations such as `do:`, `collect:`, `select:`, and `reject:` instead of explicit `for` loops whenever possible. These operations are generally optimized for performance by the Smalltalk VM.

- Minimize the loop body's workload by moving invariant code outside the loop. Invariant code is the code that does not depend on the loop variable and therefore, needs to be executed only once.

- Avoid unnecessary collection copying within loops. If the collection does not change during iteration, reference it directly.

Example: Loop Optimization

Let's consider an example where we optimize a loop using collection operations:

```
"A suboptimal loop"
suboptimalResult := OrderedCollection new.
1 to: 10000 do: [:i |
    (i even) ifTrue: [suboptimalResult add: i]].

"Optimized using select:"
optimizedResult := (1 to: 10000) select: [:i | i even].
```

In this example, the optimized variant uses `select:` to filter even numbers from a range, which is more concise and performs better than manually iterating and checking each number.

Collection Handling Techniques

Proper handling and manipulation of collections can also contribute significantly to the performance of Smalltalk applications. Below are some techniques for optimizing collection handling:

- When the size of a collection is known in advance, use `new:` method to initialize it with the exact capacity. This avoids the overhead of dynamically resizing the collection.

- Use specific collection types judiciously. For instance, use `OrderedCollection` for collections requiring insertion order preservation and `Set` for collections needing fast membership testing without duplicate elements.

- Consider lazily initialized collections (via `streams` or `lazy` collections) to defer computation until needed, especially for large datasets.

Benchmarking Optimizations

After applying optimizations, it is crucial to benchmark the performance improvements. Smalltalk provides tools like `TimeProfiler` and `MessageTally` to profile execution time and message sends, respectively. It is advisable to measure both before and after optimization to quantify the performance gains.

Here is an example of simple benchmarking using `Time millisecondsToRun:`:

```
timeTaken := Time millisecondsToRun: [
    optimizedResult := (1 to: 10000) select: [:i | i even]].
Transcript show: 'Time taken: ', timeTaken printString, ' ms'.
```

By paying attention to loop and collection optimization, along with diligent profiling, Smalltalk developers can achieve significant performance improvements in their applications. The key is to choose the right strategy based on the problem at hand and constantly quantify the impact of optimizations through rigorous benchmarking.

10.7 Using Caches and Memoization to Improve Performance

Caching and memoization are powerful techniques to enhance the performance of Smalltalk applications by avoiding redundant computations. While they share a common goal, their approaches and implementation nuances vary significantly. This section will dissect both strategies, illustrating how they can be effectively leveraged in Smalltalk to optimize application performance.

Understanding Caching

Caching refers to the storage of result data generated from expensive operations. When the same operation is requested in the future, the cached result is returned instead of recalculating it. This can significantly reduce execution time, especially for operations that are computationally intensive or rely on slow I/O operations.

Implementing caching in Smalltalk involves creating a cache object or data structure that stores result data keyed by the parameters of the operation. Below is an example demonstrating a simple method cache in Smalltalk:

```
MyClass>>cachedMethod: anArgument
  | cacheKey result |
  cacheKey := anArgument asString.
  result := Cache at: cacheKey ifAbsent: [
    | computationResult |
    computationResult := self expensiveOperation: anArgument.
    Cache at: cacheKey put: computationResult.
    computationResult
  ].
  ^result
```

In this example, the `Cache` is a dictionary where each key is the string representation of an argument, and the value is the result of the expensive operation. The `cachedMethod:` first checks if the result for the given argument exists in the `Cache`. If not, it performs the operation and stores the result in the `Cache` before returning it.

Leveraging Memoization

Memoization is a specific form of caching that applies to functions with pure output; that is, the output is entirely determined by the input. It memorizes the result of function calls based on the function's parameters, and if the function is called again with the same parameters, the memorized result is returned.

In Smalltalk, memoization can be achieved by wrapping the function or method logic within a closure that maintains a local cache. Below is an example of memoizing a factorial computation in Smalltalk:

```
memoizedFactorial := [:n |
```

```
  | memo |
  memo := Dictionary new.
  memo at: 0 put: 1; at: 1 put: 1.
  (memo at: n ifAbsentPut: [
    n * (self value: n - 1)
  ])
].
```

In this example, a dictionary `memo` is used to store the factorial results keyed by their argument. If the function is called with a particular argument, it first checks if the result is in `memo`. If not, it computes the result, stores it in `memo`, and returns it. This significantly reduces the number of recursive calls for large values of `n`.

Impact of Caching and Memoization on Performance

Both caching and memoization can dramatically improve the performance of Smalltalk applications, especially those with a significant amount of redundant or computationally expensive operations. However, developers should be judicious in their use, as maintaining caches, especially large ones, can increase memory consumption. It is crucial to strike a balance between the performance improvements from caching and the memory overhead incurred.

Furthermore, the effectiveness of caching and memoization strategies depends on the application's specific workload. They are most effective when there are a high number of repeated operations with the same inputs. Profiling tools discussed in earlier sections can be used to identify such hotspots in your application where caching and memoization could be most beneficial.

Caching and memoization are potent techniques in the Smalltalk developer's toolkit for optimizing application performance. By understanding and applying these strategies wisely, developers can significantly reduce the execution time of their applications while managing the trade-offs in memory usage.

10.8 Concurrency in Smalltalk: Processes and Threads

Concurrency is a pivotal concept in modern computing that involves executing multiple sequences of operations simultaneously. In Smalltalk, this is predominantly managed through processes and threads. This section will elucidate the mechanisms Smalltalk provides for concurrency, detailing how to effectively utilize processes and threads, the nuances between them, and best practices for synchronization and communication.

Smalltalk conceptualizes concurrency through the notion of "Processes". A Process in Smalltalk can be thought of as an independent sequence of actions (a thread of execution) that runs in the same shared memory space as other processes. Smalltalk's processes are lightweight compared to operating system processes and more akin to threads in other programming languages; however, for historical reasons and consistency within the Smalltalk community, they are referred to as "Processes".

Creating and Managing Processes

A new process in Smalltalk can be initiated by creating an instance of the `BlockClosure` class and sending it the `#fork` message. Here is an example:

```
[Transcript show: 'This code runs in a separate process'] fork.
```

This will create a new process that executes the code within the block closure asynchronously. The parent process, typically the main UI or application process, will continue executing without waiting for the newly forked process to complete.

Process Scheduling

Smalltalk's virtual machine incorporates a scheduler to manage the execution of multiple processes. By default, processes are scheduled preemptively based on priority levels. Every process is assigned a priority when it is created, and the scheduler executes processes in a descending order of their priority.

Priorities range from 1 (lowest) to 10 (highest), with the main UI process typically running at a default priority of 8. To change a process's priority, use the `#priority:` method, as shown below:

```
myProcess priority: 7.
```

A process with a higher priority can interrupt a lower-priority process, but two processes of the same priority level will share execution time, effectively achieving cooperative multitasking.

Synchronization and Communication

Synchronization and communication between processes in Smalltalk are crucial for ensuring data integrity and preventing race conditions. Smalltalk provides several mechanisms for this, including Semaphores, Conditions, and Monitors.

A Semaphore is a low-level synchronization tool that can be used to control access to shared resources. The following example demonstrates how a semaphore can be used to synchronize access to a shared resource:

```
| semaphore resource |
semaphore := Semaphore new.
resource := SharedResource new.

[semaphore critical: [resource use]] fork.
[semaphore critical: [resource use]] fork.
```

In this example, the `critical:` method ensures that only one process at a time can execute the block of code that uses the shared resource, thus preventing concurrent access.

Concurrency in Smalltalk, managed through processes and employing synchronization mechanisms like Semaphores, Conditions, and Monitors, enables developers to write robust, multitasking applications. Understanding how to effectively leverage these tools is key to optimizing application performance and ensuring data integrity in concurrent execution contexts. Developers are encouraged to familiarize themselves with these concepts and apply them judiciously to harness the full potential of Smalltalk in creating responsive and efficient applications.

10.9 Networking and I/O Optimization

Optimizing network-related operations and Input/Output (I/O) processes is vital for improving the performance and responsiveness of Smalltalk applications that interact with external resources or services. This segment sheds light on strategies to enhance networking and I/O operations, ensuring efficient data transmission and minimizing latency.

Reducing Network Latency

Network latency significantly impacts application performance, particularly in distributed systems or web-based applications. To mitigate this, consider the following approaches:

- **Use Persistent Connections:** Re-establishing connections for each request incurs overhead. Persistent connections reduce latency by reusing existing connections for multiple requests.
- **Compress Data:** Sending compressed data over the network can decrease transmission time. Smalltalk provides utilities for data compression and decompression, which should be leveraged when handling large datasets.
- **Batch Requests:** Whenever feasible, batch multiple requests into a single one to reduce the number of round-trips needed. This is particularly effective in scenarios where the application requires data from several sources.

Optimizing I/O Operations

I/O operations, especially disk I/O, can be a bottleneck in applications managing large volumes of data. To optimize I/O performance, consider these strategies:

- **Asynchronous I/O:** Utilize asynchronous I/O operations to prevent blocking the main application thread while waiting for I/O operations to complete. Smalltalk's native support for asynchronous programming can be effectively used here.

- **Caching:** Implement caching mechanisms to temporarily store frequently accessed data in memory. This can dramatically reduce the number of costly disk I/O operations.

- **Buffering:** Applying buffering techniques allows consolidating smaller I/O operations into larger chunks. This reduces the overhead caused by frequent system calls for reading or writing data.

Leveraging Protocols and Serialization

Optimizing the choice of network protocols and data serialization formats is crucial for minimizing overhead and efficiently utilizing bandwidth.

- **Protocol Selection:** Choose the right protocol based on the application's requirements. For instance, UDP may be more suitable than TCP for scenarios where speed is prioritized over reliability.

- **Efficient Serialization:** Select a compact and fast serialization format to minimize the size of the data being transmitted. Smalltalk supports various serialization formats, and choosing the right one can significantly affect performance.

Implementing Network Caching and Compression

Integrating caching and compression mechanisms at the network layer can enhance performance by reducing the amount of data transmitted and decreasing server response times.

```
"Example of data compression in Smalltalk"
| data compressedData |
data := 'This is a string that will be compressed'.
compressedData := ZipArchive new compress: data.
```

```
Output example is omitted since this operation occurs in memory.
```

Profiling Network and I/O Performance

Regular profiling of network and I/O operations is essential to identify bottlenecks and optimize accordingly. Tools and utilities available within the Smalltalk environment enable developers to monitor and analyze the performance of these operations, guiding targeted optimization efforts.

```
"Example of profiling network operations"
| profiler results |
profiler := MessageTally spyOn: [self performNetworkOperations].
results := profiler report.
```

```
- 75% performNetworkOperations
- 25% other operations
```

By applying the outlined strategies, developers can significantly enhance the networking and I/O performance of their Smalltalk applications. These optimizations contribute to a more responsive and efficient application, improving overall user satisfaction.

10.10 Writing Efficient Code: Best Practices and Pitfalls

Efficiency in code writing is not just about enhancing performance; it's about writing code that is maintainable, understandable, and scalable. In the context of Smalltalk, an object-oriented programming language known for its simplicity and elegance, writing efficient code encompasses adhering to best practices while avoiding common pitfalls. This section will thoroughly examine these aspects to guide developers in optimizing their Smalltalk applications effectively.

First and foremost, understand that in Smalltalk, everything is an object, and interactions happen through message passing. This foundational concept influences how one should approach performance optimization and memory management.

Best Practices

Let's delve into the best practices for writing efficient Smalltalk code:

- **Use Polymorphism wisely:** Rather than relying on conditional statements like if-else or switch, employ polymorphism. It not only improves the readability and maintainability of the code but also enhances performance by utilizing dynamic dispatch efficiently.

- **Minimize message passing in tight loops:** Message passing is a powerful feature of Smalltalk but can become a bottleneck in performance-critical sections of the code, especially within loops. Precompute values outside loops and use local variables to hold these values to reduce the overhead.

```
"Example of minimizing message passing in a loop:"
sum := 0.
collectionSize := aCollection size.
1 to: collectionSize do: [:index |
   sum := sum + (aCollection at: index).
].
```

- **Utilize built-in collection methods:** Smalltalk provides a rich set of powerful collection methods that are optimized for performance. Whenever possible, use these methods instead of manually iterating over collections.

- **Effective use of caching and memoization:** When a function is called repeatedly with the same arguments, consider caching its result to avoid recalculating it. This technique can significantly improve performance in computation-heavy applications.
- **Leverage concurrency for performance:** Smalltalk's model for concurrency, using Processes, can be utilized to perform multiple operations in parallel, thus reducing the overall execution time for performance-critical applications.

Pitfalls to Avoid

While optimizing your Smalltalk code, watch out for these common pitfalls:

- **Over-optimization:** Remember the adage, "premature optimization is the root of all evil." Do not optimize without profiling and understanding where the actual bottlenecks are.
- **Ignoring the Garbage Collector:** Smalltalk's garbage collector helps manage memory efficiently, but overly frequent allocations and deallocations can stress it, leading to performance degradation. Be mindful of your object creation and destruction patterns.
- **Misusing Collections:** Choosing the wrong type of collection for a particular use case can lead to suboptimal performance. Understand the characteristics of different collection types and select them judiciously.
- **Neglecting Smalltalk idioms and conventions:** Smalltalk has a rich and expressive syntax that, when used correctly, can greatly enhance code clarity and performance. Ignoring these idioms can result in code that is difficult to read, maintain, and optimize.

```
"Example of a common misuse of collections:"
result := OrderedCollection new.
1 to: 10000 do: [:i | result add: i].
```

Note: This can be replaced with `result := (1 to: 10000) asOrderedCollection`, which is more efficient and idiomatic.

Writing efficient Smalltalk code is a balance between leveraging the language's features and adhering to best practices. By understanding and avoiding common pitfalls, developers can ensure their code is not only performant but also readable and maintainable.

10.11 Advanced Techniques: JIT Compilation and VM Tuning

In Smalltalk performance optimization, understanding and implementing just-in-time (JIT) compilation techniques, along with virtual machine (VM) tuning, are of paramount importance. These aspects offer compelling pathways to significantly boosting the execution speed of Smalltalk programs by optimizing at the bytecode and VM level.

Just-In-Time (JIT) Compilation in Smalltalk

JIT compilation refers to the dynamic compilation of bytecode into native machine code at runtime. This contrasts with the traditional approach where the entire source code is compiled into machine code before execution, known as ahead-of-time (AOT) compilation. The JIT compiler translates bytecode, which is a set of platform-independent instructions specific to Smalltalk, into a platform-specific machine code. The primary benefit of JIT compilation is that it can optimize execution dynamically based on runtime information, which is not available at compile time.

In Smalltalk, the JIT compilation process entails several critical steps:

- Monitoring the execution of bytecode to identify hot spots, which are code segments executed frequently.
- Translating the identified bytecode into native machine code.

- Optimizing the generated machine code for performance, utilizing runtime execution data.

- Storing the optimized machine code in a method cache for subsequent executions, thereby avoiding re-compilation.

To illustrate the JIT compilation, consider the following Smalltalk code snippet:

```
Smalltalk defineClass: #Fibonacci
    superclass: #{Core.Object}
    indexedType: #none
    private: false
    instanceVariableNames: ''
    classInstanceVariableNames: ''
    imports: ''
    category: ''.

Fibonacci class >> computeFibonacci: n
    ^(n <= 2)
        ifTrue: [1]
        ifFalse: [(self computeFibonacci: n - 1) + (self computeFibonacci: n - 2)
            ].
```

In this example, the method `computeFibonacci:` is likely to be a hot spot, especially for larger values of `n`, due to its recursive nature. The JIT compiler can optimize this method by translating it into optimized native machine code, which reduces execution time significantly.

Virtual Machine (VM) Tuning

VM tuning encompasses a set of techniques and configurations aimed at optimizing the runtime environment for performance. In the context of Smalltalk, VM tuning involves adjusting various parameters and settings of the Smalltalk VM to enhance execution efficiency.

Some key aspects of VM tuning include:

- Memory management configuration, such as the size of young and old generations in the garbage-collected heap.

- JIT compilation settings, including the method inlining threshold and the size of the method cache.

- Adjusting the VM's thread and process priorities to align with the application's requirements.

- Tweaking the garbage collection strategy to balance throughput with pause times.

Adjusting these parameters requires careful analysis and understanding of both the application's behavior and the VM's performance characteristics. Profiling tools, as discussed in earlier sections, can provide invaluable insights for this purpose.

To demonstrate VM tuning's impact, consider the memory management adjustments. By increasing the size of the young generation space, objects are more likely to be allocated and collected within this space, which is usually faster than collecting from the older generation. Such a tweak could be beneficial for applications with high object churn, improving overall execution speed.

JIT compilation and VM tuning are advanced techniques that can significantly enhance the performance of Smalltalk applications. These strategies require a deep understanding of both the application's runtime behavior and the VM's architecture. By effectively leveraging JIT compilation, developers can optimize the execution of hot spots in their code. Simultaneously, VM tuning allows for the customization of the runtime environment to meet the specific performance needs of an application. Together, these techniques enable developers to push the boundaries of Smalltalk performance, ensuring that applications remain responsive and efficient under various conditions.

10.12 Debugging Performance Issues in Smalltalk

Debugging performance issues requires a systematic approach to identify and resolve bottlenecks within Smalltalk applications. This section will discuss practical strategies and tools that developers can employ to diagnose and address performance problems, ensuring that their Smalltalk applications run efficiently.

Firstly, understanding the common sources of performance bottlenecks is essential. These can broadly be categorized into CPU-bound issues, where the program consumes excessive processor time, and memory-bound issues, where the program uses memory inefficiently. In Smalltalk, performance issues often arise from inefficient message passing, excessive garbage collection, and suboptimal use of collections and loops.

To effectively debug performance issues, developers should start by profiling their application. Profiling involves measuring the resource usage of a program, such as CPU time and memory allocation, to identify hotspots or sections of the code that are consuming disproportionate resources. Smalltalk provides several tools for profiling, one of which is the `MessageTally` class.

```
MessageTally spyOn: [YourCodeHere].
```

The above code snippet demonstrates how to use `MessageTally` to profile a block of Smalltalk code. `MessageTally` reports the time spent in each method, allowing developers to pinpoint which methods are performance bottlenecks.

Once the bottlenecks are identified, the next step is to optimize the problematic code sections. For instance, if a method is identified as a bottleneck due to heavy usage of list processing, developers can explore optimizing the collection handling. This might involve switching to more efficient collection types, employing lazy evaluation, or batch processing techniques.

In addition to profiling, developers can employ tracing to gain insights into the execution flow of their applications. Tracing records the sequence of message sends and method executions, helping developers understand how their code runs over time. While tracing is more granular and comprehensive than profiling, it also generates a considerable amount of data, which can be challenging to analyze.

```
YourClass>>yourMethod
    self trace.
    "Your method implementation here."
```

In the snippet above, invoking the `trace` method within a method logs each message send during the execution of `yourMethod`, aiding in diagnosing performance issues related to message passing.

Effective debugging of performance issues also involves understanding Smalltalk's memory model, particularly garbage collection. Developers should monitor the frequency and duration of garbage collection cycles, as excessive garbage collection can significantly impact application performance. Tools such as `VMStatistics` can provide valuable information on memory usage and garbage collection metrics.

```
GC stats - total: 500ms, max pause: 50ms
```

The output example above shows a summary of garbage collection statistics, highlighting the total time spent on garbage collection and the maximum pause time.

Lastly, it is crucial to adopt an iterative approach to debugging performance issues: profile the application, identify bottlenecks, apply optimizations, and repeat the process as necessary. Additionally, seeking feedback from the Smalltalk community and consulting documentation can provide insights into best practices for performance optimization.

By leveraging profiling and tracing tools, understanding the underlying memory model, and applying targeted optimizations, developers can effectively debug and enhance the performance of their Smalltalk applications.

10.13 Case Studies: Real-world Optimization Examples

Expounding upon theoretical strategies and techniques for performance optimization and memory management is foundational. However, the application of these principles in real-world scenarios elucidates their practical impact and the nuances involved in effectively deploying them. This section presents comprehensive case studies to demonstrate how optimization strategies were executed in Smalltalk applications, offering insights into challenges faced and the solutions derived.

Case Study 1: E-Commerce Application

The first case study involves a Smalltalk-based e-commerce application that experienced significant slowdowns during peak shopping hours. Initial profiling, using the MessageTally class, indicated that the bottlenecks were primarily in the product search functionality and the checkout process.

- The product search function was heavily reliant on iterating through collections of product objects to match search criteria. By replacing generic collections with hashed collections, and optimizing the hashing function for product objects, the search speed was significantly improved.

```
"Optimization of Product Search"
products := products as: HashedCollection.
```

- The checkout process, involving multiple message passing between objects for calculating discounts, taxes, and shipping, was streamlined by reducing the number of messages passed. This was achieved by integrating these calculations within fewer, more comprehensive methods.

```
"Streamlining Checkout Process"
checkoutTotal := self calculateTotalWithDiscounts: discounts Taxes:
    taxRates Shipping: shippingOptions.
```

Pre and post-optimization profiling showed a reduction in execution time by 45% during product search and 30% in the checkout process.

Case Study 2: Financial Analysis Tool

The second case involves a financial analysis tool used for real-time stock market analysis. The application suffered from long garbage collection pauses and memory overflow errors during high-volume trading periods.

The optimization strategy focused on memory management, specifically in the management of temporary objects created during analysis.

- A significant reduction in temporary object creation was achieved by reusing objects wherever possible, especially those involved in analytical computations.

```
"Reuse of Analytical Objects"
if not (TempHolder includesKey: #analysisObject) then
    [TempHolder at: #analysisObject put: (AnalyzeTool new: dataSize)].
analysisResult := (TempHolder at: #analysisObject) runAnalysis: dataSet.
```

- Fine-tuning the garbage collector settings based on the application's usage pattern led to more efficient memory management, reducing the frequency and duration of garbage collection pauses.

The application's performance improved, with a 60% reduction in memory-related errors and a more fluid user experience during peak activity.

Through these case studies, it's elucidated that the application of Smalltalk performance optimization and memory management strategies can lead to substantial improvements in application responsiveness and stability. Profiling tools are indispensable for identifying bottlenecks, and a combination of optimizing message passing, collection handling, and memory management can address the myriad challenges faced in real-world applications.

www.ingramcontent.com/pod-product-compliance
Lightning Source LLC
Chambersburg PA
CBHW070937050326
40689CB00014B/3246